PSYCHOLOGY
AND THE SOCIAL PATTERN

INTERNATIONAL LIBRARY OF SOCIOLOGY
AND SOCIAL RECONSTRUCTION

Founded by Karl Mannheim

Editor : W. J. H. Sprott

PSYCHOLOGY
AND THE SOCIAL PATTERN

by

JULIAN BLACKBURN

Ph.D. (Cantab.), B.Sc. (Econ.)

LECTURER IN SOCIAL PSYCHOLOGY AT THE LONDON
SCHOOL OF ECONOMICS AND POLITICAL SCIENCE,
UNIVERSITY OF LONDON

LONDON

ROUTLEDGE & KEGAN PAUL LTD

BROADWAY HOUSE: 68-74 CARTER LANE, E.C.4

First published 1945
Second impression 1945
Third impression 1948
Fourth impression 1950
Fifth impression 1953
Sixth impression 1961

To

F. C. BARTLETT

Printed in Great Britain by Butler & Tanner Ltd., Frome and London

CONTENTS

PREFACE

Different psychologists with their varied approaches and interests have fostered the development of psychology in many different directions. From each of the principal developers psychology has gained a great deal. Sometimes the gains have carried with them certain elements of disadvantage, as when the followers of the original exponent of a doctrine have been led away by their ardour to ignore the contributions of those with whose views they disagree, but on balance the gain to psychology as a whole by the divergence of views of its exponents has been considerable.

My own prejudices and antipathies will probably become obvious to the reader as he wends (or ploughs) his way through this book. I should prefer to leave it to him to discover them for himself rather than to make out a list of all those of which I am consciously aware. I must, however, make a few comments about some of them which have importantly influenced the choice of topics in, and the arrangement of, the book.

I have attempted to give some account of most of the major contributions to experimental psychology and to introduce these contributions into those parts of the book where they seemed to be most relevant, but what has influenced me more than anything else has been an attempt to bring out the *social* aspects of those topics which are generally discussed in textbooks on psychology, and also to try to forge a link between the topics usually confined to textbooks on general psychology and those which are more usually discussed in textbooks on abnormal psychology. At first I intended to write a textbook on social psychology, but as the planning of the book proceeded I felt that it was first of all necessary to see how far the social aspects of general and abnormal psychology could be explored. Then, having cleared the ground, I could proceed, as I hope to do, to discuss the social framework into which human beings are born—the effect on their behaviour of heredity, race, sex, class and family life—and then to discuss the social relationships which impinge upon and influence their behaviour in society. These topics I hope to discuss in two forthcoming books.

One chapter heading which is found in practically every textbook on psychology has not been included in this book.

That is a chapter on learning. The reasons for this are first that part of what I have to say on the subject is to be found in the chapter on motivation, and secondly that I hope to deal with the topic in much greater detail (in so far as it concerns human beings) in a future book on developmental psychology.

This book, therefore, should be regarded as the first part of an attempt to estimate the interaction between the individual and society. I hope and believe that the topics and the treatment hang together sufficiently closely for it to be able to stand on its own, but I have constantly held at the back of my mind a picture of its relationship to the other topics which I have planned to discuss in the future.

*   *   *

I would like to thank Professor Morris Ginsberg for the trouble he has taken in reading through the entire script and in making valuable comments on it. It was he and L. T. Hobhouse who first introduced me to, and interested me in, social psychology many years ago. I was subsequently influenced very considerably by the ideas of Kurt Koffka with whom I worked in America, thanks to the generosity of the Rockefeller Foundation, and by the extension of the Gestalt views to social psychology which is implicit in the books of Ruth Benedict, Margaret Mead and Otto Klineberg. On the clinical side I am indebted to the wisdom and stimulation of Dr. Aubrey Lewis with whom I worked at the Maudsley Hospital.

The greatest debt of all during the past fifteen years I owe to the inspiring leadership and constant encouragement of Professor F. C. Bartlett to whom I dedicate this book in gratitude and affection.

HADSTOCK, ESSEX.
May, 1944.

PSYCHOLOGY AND THE SOCIAL PATTERN

CHAPTER I

INTRODUCTION

People behave in all manner of ways. Sometimes their behaviour is the result of the influences which have impinged on them in the small family group, the bigger school group, or the still bigger institutional or national groups in which they have been brought up. Each of these groups has its own manners and customs, traditions and conventions, and these are so strong that the single individual is often swamped by them if he tries to behave in a way which is contrary to them. More often he simply accepts them as the proper way to behave.

Let us take as an example of this what might happen to a person who enters one of the great professions, let us say the army. It may sometimes happen that a young man entering the army finds a number of ways of behaving that he cannot understand. With his natural impetuosity and his desire to get things done quickly, and with his necessarily incomplete knowledge of all the facts, he cannot understand the delay that sometimes occurs in coming to decisions. But these decisions may have a whole host of implications about which he is completely unaware. The applications and the requests for this and that which have to be made through the " proper channels " originally at any rate had some reason behind them, though the exact reason may not be quite clear even to the young man's superior officers. All this sort of thing, therefore, he wants to alter : it appears to him to be nothing more than pig-headed obstinacy on the part of an antiquated, perhaps even prehistoric, animal. But having only just entered the army himself he does not possess any power to make the alterations he desires. He decides, however, that as soon as he has reached a responsible position he will make a clean sweep of all these hindrances and go down to history as the man who brought the army up to date. But what in fact usually happens to a young man like this ? As he works his way up to positions of greater power he not only

begins to see some of the reasons why the formal channels are sometimes the best, but he also tends to become so imbued with the general army atmosphere and way of doing things that he begins to think quite genuinely that it is the best way. Besides, by the time he is reaching a position of real power he is getting a good deal older, and his youthful impetuosity and ardour are becoming somewhat dulled and dimmer. He no longer wants to do things quite so quickly and feverishly as he did when he first joined up. All these factors—particularly, perhaps, the assimilation of the military manners and customs, conventions and traditions—lead him into the position of *not wanting* to make those radical changes that he wanted to make when he was younger. The institution of the army has affected his behaviour in an extremely important way.

This kind of thing really belongs to the province of social psychology, and one of the first things that this book attempts to do is to try to pick out from the topics which the general psychologists have written about and described, those aspects which have a bearing on the problems of social psychology. What is there in general psychology that is of interest and use to the social psychologist? Can we find any indication in the facts about perceiving, thinking, remembering, ability, temperament, motivation and emotion which the general psychologists have described so often and so fully of the way in which the groups or cultural patterns in which people have been brought up are affecting those people's behaviour in these respects? That is the first problem.

A second problem is that though most people will have their behaviour modified by the groups to which they belong, yet there will always remain some people who in spite of (or sometimes because of) the traditions and customs, manners and conventions of their groups, behave in ways which conflict with those mores. Such people tend to become the maladjusted individuals in their groups, the deviants from the usual ways of behaving. What we have to do in the second place, therefore, is to see whether a link can be forged between the normal ways of behaving, which are the general psychologist's province, and the abnormal, maladjusted ways which are usually described in books on psychiatry. What we shall try to do is to investigate the relationship between " normal " and " abnormal " behaviour. Once again our starting point is the point of view of the general psychologist.

PERCEIVING

There are various factors which may be regarded as objective and which influence the way in which things are perceived. These partly depend on the structure of the eye or the ear, the nerve endings in the retina and other sense organs, the fact that we have two eyes, and other physiological conditions of this kind. Then there are factors which have been studied in detail by psychologists which depend on the stimuli themselves—things like the strength or the size of the stimuli, the way in which they are grouped, their similarity and so on. But in addition to these objective conditions there are a number of subjective conditions. Some of these depend principally on the influence of a person's social environment, and some depend to a more important degree on the temperamental make-up of the individual himself. It is at these two points, therefore, that we may look for the link between, on the one hand, general psychology and social psychology and, on the other hand, between general psychology and abnormal psychology in so far as perceiving is concerned. Thus some of the experimenters on perceiving have shown that in many perceptions there is a degree of inference. Now the kind of inference that is drawn may mainly depend on the fact that in a particular group of people it is customary to infer in a particular way (e.g. that when one is alone in a house at midnight with the wind howling outside, any creaking floorboards or sudden unexpected sounds are being made by someone or something with an evil and hostile intention against one) : or it may mainly depend on one's own peculiar temperamental and emotional make-up (e.g. to take an extreme example, that a ring at the bell at midday when the sun is shining brightly out of doors, and one has one's family about one, portends the arrival of a horrid hunchback, dressed in red and with a cleft foot).

Perceptions which principally depend on objective factors are, so far as we can judge, usually seen in the same way by everybody, and this is true also of those illusions which depend on a particular kind of physiological stimulation for their appearance. Anyone who perceives them perceives them in the same kind of way, though in fact the way they are seen is different from what they really are. Other perceptions depending principally on social factors are also fairly generally shared within that particular community. But there are still others which

are far more individual, depending on a person's particular interests and attitudes. These range all the way from a tendency to perceive more of a particular kind of object than most people whose interests have not been developed along these lines, through illusions and hallucinations to delusions or false beliefs. It is often very difficult to draw a precise line of demarcation between these different types of behaviour, e.g. to say whether a particular piece of behaviour is a false perception or a false belief. Thus it might be more accurate to classify the example of the inference that a ring at the bell portended the arrival of a devil as a false belief rather than as a false perception. But for reasons that will be found in Chapter II I think that these two types of behaviour are closely connected.

BELIEFS

Beliefs as well as perceptions depend on both social and on individual factors. There is a tendency in Western civilisation to believe things to be true when they fit in and agree with the existing logically coherent system of facts. There is in many respects a social pressure towards scientific and experimentally established facts. But there are in addition a number of social pressures of a more emotional kind. In primitive communities these are much more widespread than in our own community. There we find numerous social pressures towards beliefs in magic, witchcraft, omens and spells. Even in Western civilisation, how-ever, there are many emotionally determined social pressures. These sometimes take the form of widespread types of wishful thinking, when, for example, a particular group is fighting for its existence. But they also take less specific forms as well. The prevalence of superstitions, even among those who have had the benefit of a scientific education, indicates how strong these tendencies may be. Most people who consciously reject a piece of superstitious behaviour, or who purposely do something which they know is running contrary to the superstition, have a slightly uncomfortable feeling as they do so, for they are then doing something which conflicts with the popular belief. Their behaviour is consciously directed against the manners and customs of their fellows, and their feeling of malaise may spontaneously arise from this cause. In these ways we can trace the influence of the beliefs of the group on the behaviour and the beliefs of the individual within it.

In other cases we can see how individual factors are of more

importance than social factors in determining a person's beliefs. This frequently happens in scientific research, giving rise to new discoveries or to new theories which conflict with the existing beliefs of the social group. In such cases the determinants of the new belief are principally based on rational grounds, and after a while it may be that the new theory passes into and among the accepted beliefs of the group. But in other cases the principal determinants of individual beliefs are emotional. Without consciously allowing himself to realise it a person has to believe certain things because he cannot face the difficult problems of adjustment to his social group if he believes otherwise. He has to believe that his neighbours are gossiping about him because he raises his sense of self-importance thereby, and he cannot face the realisation of his true insignificance. Sometimes these emotionally-determined beliefs reach a fantastic degree of complexity, as in the systematised delusions of schizophrenic patients. In these one often sees a train of thought worked out with faultless logic to a towering height of elaboration, without the individual being able to appreciate the fact that though he has drawn perfectly correct conclusions from his premises, yet those premises themselves are hopelessly inaccurate. Thus if a patient believes that the Chief Rabbi, the Minister of Labour, the proprietor of the *Daily Express*, and the managing director of Nobel Industries are jointly engaged in a plot to hound him from his job it will be possible for him to associate the most trifling annoyances of his daily life with one or other of these eminent gentlemen and to defend the association with convincing argument. Given his implicit belief in his premises the association of necessity follows. And anyone who does his best to cure the patient of his delusion will be in danger of being immediately regarded as an agent of his enemies, for one thing the patient must avoid at all cost (though he does not consciously realise it himself) is the painful process of readjusting himself socially. The quickest way to rid himself of the unwelcome attempts of a doctor to cure him is to classify him at once as a hostile agent. Then it is no longer necessary to pay any attention to what he says.

Sometimes the individual and false beliefs arise through inadequacies in a person's intellectual make-up. In such cases his beliefs may be based more on rational than on emotional grounds, but his intellectual deficiencies lead him to the wrong conclusions. Such may be seen in cases of intellectual impairment due, let us say, to gunshot wounds in the head or to organic

deterioration as the result of alcoholic intoxication, syphilitic infection or senility. Or they may be due to an innate lack of mental ability, to a mental defect which prevents a person from developing his ideas and thoughts to the same degree of complexity as other people.

Thus in thinking, as in perceiving, a relationship may be discovered between the provinces of the general psychologist and those of the social psychologist and of the psychiatrist.

REMEMBERING

The same thing is true of remembering. Recent experimental work has brought out the importance of the processes of inference and of construction in all attempts to remember. These processes are as much affected by the forces arising within a person's social group and by those which result from his own peculiar temperamental and intellectual make-up as are the corresponding processes in perceiving and in thinking.

The influence of the social group on the kind of things remembered and on the number of things remembered is an aspect of anthropology and of folk-lore that has not at the present time been developed very far. Such work as there is, however, indicates that there are very important and very interesting differences between different social groups, with different traditions and ways of life, and the kind of things that are remembered as well as on the total amount remembered.

More material exists on the individual aspects of the matter. It can be shown that individuals with different temperamental and emotional make-ups show marked differences in the quality and quantity of the things they remember, and when one passes beyond what is usually regarded as lying within the normal range of divergence from the average, when one passes to the patients who are suffering from impairment of their mental processes, one sees at once the importance of the constructive processes in remembering. Many of these patients show disturbances of remembering which closely resemble delusional symptoms. Thus a patient may describe a visit he has recently paid to the landlady in whose house he lived for many years, and say that as he went away at the end of the visit the little kitten to which he had been very attached when he was living there sat up on its hind legs and put its front paws to its eyes to catch the tears that were pouring down its cheeks. But as the disturbances in their mental processes mainly affect things which

are remembered it is more convenient to consider them under this heading than under disturbances of systems of ideas and beliefs. Nevertheless here again the precise line of demarcation is very difficult to draw.

Just as some false beliefs are principally determined by emotional causes and others by intellectual inadequacies, so too there are impairments in memory which are due more to emotional than to intellectual limitations. Just as we sometimes believe what we want to believe, so too we sometimes forget what we want to forget. This may concern a relatively unimportant matter, such as a dentist's appointment, or, in a more extreme form, it may take the shape of a hysterical loss of memory embracing an inability to remember one's own name, to recognise one's relations or one's own home, etc. In such cases some fairly obvious situation from which the patient wishes to escape can usually be discovered by the psychiatrist, though the patient himself will not consciously admit its existence.

ABILITY

When we turn to ability and intelligence it seems at first difficult to see how different social environments can possibly affect them. Yet we do not have to look far before we realise that though the social environment cannot increase the amount of a person's intellectual endowment, it may considerably affect the extent to which he can make full use of the amount of ability he possesses. It is quite possible for a person with an excellent native endowment never to have an opportunity to develop his potentialities to the full, because he has never been in an environment which will allow them to develop. The point is even more important when one considers the results of intelligence tests, for intelligence tests are regarded by many people as fairly accurate measures of the amount of native intelligence a person possesses. Yet there is a large amount of experimental evidence to show that the ability to answer intelligence test questions is affected very considerably by the kind of environment in which a person is brought up.[1] This is particularly the case with tests which are based on language and the use of words, for verbal facility or relative literacy is affected to an important degree by the kind and amount of education a person receives. But it is also true of tests which are not based on language. This is not to say that

---

[1] Apart from some of the evidence that is mentioned in Chapter 5 a great deal more will be found in my forthcoming book, *The Framework of Human Behaviour.*

intelligence tests are of no practical value. On the contrary they are of very considerable use when the people being compared are known to have had a very similar background of education and experiences. They are particularly useful in indicating the relative degree to which children in the same school or in the same types of school have benefited by their education. But their limitations should never be overlooked when one is trying to make a comparison between the innate abilities of people—particularly adults—who have been subjected to the influences of widely different social groups. Thus when one applies intelligence tests to groups of people of widely different ages in order to try to get a picture of the growth and decline of intelligence with age it is impossible to pick out from a decline in test scores in the later age groups the relative importance of a decline in interest in the kind of things that the test questions ask about, the different effects on different people of the habits and interests of different social groups, or the real decline in innate ability due to the natural processes of mental impairment as the result of old age.

In these ways therefore it is possible to trace the influence of the social group on intelligence test scores.

It is also possible to trace the relationship between " normal " and " abnormal " ability. When abnormality consists of an excessive degree of verbal facility a person tends to be regarded as extremely brilliant and his intelligence test score is usually very high. But if his asymmetry in mental development has taken a different direction, if, for example, he is an almost illiterate mechanical genius, he may find himself incarcerated in a home for mental defectives. Our social group attaches such overwhelming importance to verbal and linguistic proficiency that it is unwilling to treat those whose abilities lie principally in other directions with the same consideration. This is not to say, of course, that some people do not have a general defect in their abilities which incapacitates them from any possibility of social adjustment. But it does, I think, imply that more attention ought to be paid to differences in types of ability and disability.

TEMPERAMENT AND TYPES

This leads us to the general question of types and temperaments. As with ability so with temperaments there is a fundamental difference between the kinds and degrees of temperamental characteristics of many people, and these may depend, in part at

least, on the balance of their glandular secretions. The influence of the social group or groups in which a person develops also frequently plays its part as well. The fact that some people look more attractive than others, or are more lively than others, means that there will be differences in the ease with which they will get on with their fellows. Those who are dull and unattractive will have to work hard to gain the social acceptance which seems to come to others quite naturally and without the expenditure of any effort. Those who are dull or unattractive may even give up the struggle and seek self-sufficiency within a very narrow circle. Thus, because they gain ready admittance to many social groups those who are bright and attractive may spontaneously develop and improve just those characteristics which increase the ease with which they get on with their fellows, and just because they have difficulty in mixing with others those who are dull and unattractive may increasingly lose confidence in their ability to get on with other people, and so find it increasingly difficult to mix with others.

So the reaction of one's social group to one's inborn characteristics may foster or discourage the development of differences in temperamental characteristics. And similarly the differences in innate temperamental endowment may materially affect the way in which people react to groups of their fellows.

MOTIVATION

When we turn to the question of motivation we find that many psychologists have defined and described a whole host of what are called *instincts*. These are usually regarded as innate patterns of behaviour which are common to all the members of the same species. But however useful the concept may be when it is used to describe certain types of behaviour in insects and birds, the traditions and customs of human groups lead to so much modification in the behaviour of their individual members that the concept can no longer be regarded as of much value for descriptive purposes so far as human beings are concerned.

Anthropologists have shown that even what are regarded as the most fundamental of human tendencies, namely maternal behaviour, sex behaviour, acquisitiveness and pugnacity are subject to considerable modification, and that in groups in which the social pattern happens to be of a certain character, the individuals within that group tend to behave in ways which conflict with these so-called fundamental tendencies. Thus in

some groups infanticide is a common practice, in others it is regarded as proper to have an equal number of boys and girls and the excess of one sex over the other is killed off, in others young adults are purchased from neighbouring tribes because it is regarded as too much trouble to bring up one's own children. Even in our own society mothers are frequently indifferent or even hostile to their children when they are born, and it is only after they have looked after them continuously for a while that they begin to appreciate their babies' individualities, to become more attached to them and to develop affectionate maternal behaviour towards them.

The cultural regulations surrounding sex behaviour also greatly modify the behaviour of men towards women. In those communities which have set up a romantic ideal men will expect quite different things from their wives and will treat them entirely differently from what will happen in communities whose ideal of women is more materialistic. Then again the social expectancy in different groups is different : in some, as in our own community, women are expected to be the gentler sex, to be less highly sexed than men and to wait for advances to be made towards them by men. But in other communities both men and women are regarded as being equally sexed, sometimes very highly sexed and sometimes very gently. And one community has been described in which the rôles that are expected of men and women in our society are apparently reversed : it is the men who wait for the women's favours to fall on them.

Many psychologists have regarded aggressiveness or pugnacity as one of the most obvious natural impulses of men, yet anthropologists have shown that the force of social conventions plays a very important part in the way in which aggressiveness is manifested. Some tribes are peace-loving and unaggressive in all aspects of their behaviour, showing no tolerance of any kind of violence and never seeking positions of responsibility and power. In others disputes are settled by verbal methods entirely ; in others the rival parties settle their dispute by being the first to break the stick with which they have to beat a tree. Thus when these types of behaviour show themselves they appear in a guise quite different from the instinctive aggressiveness or pugnacity which one can describe with such a high degree of specificity in the behaviour of most animals towards others.

Again, acquisitiveness is often merely a reflection of social conventions. Even in our own society it has been shown that

the collecting mania has become much less prevalent among young people within the last fifty years as the number of other possible ways of spending one's time and the number of other available amusements has increased. But apart from this there is a wealth of evidence available in comparative anthropology which shows that acquisitiveness is often only incidental : it is the socially acceptable way of gaining a position of prestige. The objects acquired are often of no intrinsic value whatever, but the fact of acquiring them prevents others from doing so, and one's own prestige is increased by the acquisition—even if the objects acquired should be merely bits of mud that that particular community happens to regard as valuable objects— while other people's is correspondingly diminished. Sometimes, in fact, things are acquired only to be disposed of again as quickly as possible. In such cases it is not the acquisition itself which gives the prestige but the rapidity with which one can dispose of the object acquired.

In all these ways therefore we can trace the influence of social customs on what are regarded as fundamental motivations, and the behaviour that emerges is entirely different in different communities. Nevertheless individual aspects of the matter are important too, for some people possess innate characteristics which diverge to so great an extent from the predominant patterns of their community that, far from being moulded by those patterns into conformity, they react against them and become the maladjusted people within that community. Yet had they been born into other communities with different cultural patterns they might have become not merely the well-balanced and perfectly adjusted members of that community, but even the leaders of the society. One must therefore regard maladjustments not solely in terms of an individual's characteristics, but also in their relationship to the customs of the community in which they happen to live.

EMOTIONAL BEHAVIOUR

One sees the same picture even more clearly in other forms of mental mechanism and in emotional behaviour. One of the commonest types of mental mechanism is some form of conscious or unconscious compensation for a real or imagined inferiority in some physical or mental respect. These compensations take many forms, some of which are subtler than others. One obvious and conscious form of compensation is the acceptance of one's

inadequacies in some respects and the concentration of one's energies in developing other and more favourable characteristics. Other, usually less conscious, forms of compensation are mechanisms for belittling other people or for raising one's own value by identifying oneself with a club or other association or institution which one values. One can in that way gain some reflected glory. Still less conscious mechanisms are to project on to other people the faults and shortcomings which one possesses oneself but is unwilling to acknowledge. We can see here, therefore, a transition from normal to abnormal mental mechanisms, a transition from a fairly general type of behaviour to a far less usual kind.

The same transition may be followed in other mental mechanisms. It often happens that as the result of an unexpected situation we find ourselves temporarily out of adjustment with our environment. We are apt in those conditions to react for the moment in ways that will bring us no nearer to adjustment. Thus if the engine of our car suddenly and unaccountably stops we are sometimes apt to react to the situation by repeatedly pressing the self-starter in the hope that it can be coaxed into life again. We may continue to press the self-starter after it ought to have become clear to us that the source of the trouble is to be sought elsewhere. This is a minor degree of persistent maladjustment which is common to many people. But there are other people who react in this persistently non-adaptive way with unfailing regularity and in circumstances that appear to us to be hopelessly inadequate as a predisposing cause. These are the deviants from the normal mode of behaviour, though their deviation may take a mild form like having to touch every paling, lamp-post, pillar box or tree as they pass it, or a more incapacitating compulsion such as having to repeat to themselves the first letters of every word in any sentence that they speak, or a socially dangerous compulsion such as Jack the Ripper may have suffered from.

In the same way a transition from normal to abnormal behaviour may be seen in the amount of emotion which an individual expresses in different situations. The emotion may be anxiety or joy or depression or any other. There are some circumstances, for example, in which most people would feel a certain amount of anxiety—quite justifiably most people would think. But there are also people who show a deep and consistent anxiety over what we regard as totally inadequate causes. Often

in these cases the object of the anxiety is transferred from an object which is the original cause of the anxiety but which the person is unwilling to admit into his conscious mind as the cause. Thus a person may worry unduly over his children, his wife, his health, his dog or his chickens, his remarks to other people, the weather, catching trains, or even whether the postman is going to forget to bring him his letters. And the original cause of the anxiety, which he will not consciously acknowledge and which is transferred on to so many different objects that it permeates most of his life, may be a deep-rooted belief in his own inadequacy for the job he happens to be doing and a fear that his employers will discover his incompetence and discharge him.

Although anxiety is one of the commonest forms of emotional over-reaction other emotions are also used. In both elation and depression, for example, we can trace a connection between the normal joys and sorrows felt by everybody with adequate cause in their life's experiences and the ravings of the manic patient or the suicidal vows of the depressive which are made without any adequate predisposing cause that we can discover.

Sometimes instead of an emotional over-reaction we find an emotional under-reaction. This gives rise to a completely different kind of picture. The person appears to be cold. He does not let himself go in situations in which other people regard it as appropriate, correct and proper to make a show of emotional behaviour. The degree to which he fails to be emotional, even in the most adequate of circumstances gives a measure of the extent of his deviation, and this may range from a mild degree of shyness to the more serious cases of apparent indifference in hysteric patients who may describe in detail the symptoms of their anæsthesias or paralyses or blindness without any flicker of overt emotion, or to the complete inaccessibility of some types of schizophrenic patient.

Here then we have seen the vast amount of individual variation that may surround emotional expression. But the differences do not turn entirely on differences in the innate characteristics which different people possess. The varied patterns of different communities also play their part in determining what is regarded as appropriate. Even within a given community what is regarded as appropriate in one section may be regarded as inappropriate in another. Thus the training and tradition in the Church produces on the whole a rather different type from that produced by the Stock Exchange, and in a community with a fairly high

degree of class differentiation the kind of emotion, the amount of emotion, and the expression of emotion which are regarded as appropriate by the different classes in given circumstances may vary very considerably. And when one looks beyond a single community and makes a comparative study of different communities, as anthropologists have done, the differences in what are regarded as appropriate are very much more apparent. The values and social expectancy of one community may be singularly inappropriate and misleading if they are applied to other communities.

Thus we may see in perceiving, thinking, remembering, ability, temperament, motivation and emotion how what has been discussed by the general psychologist may be linked up with the main interests of both the psychiatrist and the social psychologist. We will now turn to each of these subjects in greater detail.

CHAPTER II

PERCEIVING, ILLUSIONS AND HALLUCINATIONS

INTRODUCTORY

What we perceive in any situation depends to a large extent on what we are attending to at the time. And what we attend to depends on a number of both subjective and objective factors. Some of the subjective factors are due to innate personality and temperamental differences. This emerged in Bartlett's experiments : [1] the cautious, hesitating person reacted quite differently in the same objective situation from the confident, positive person ; and the person in a doubting mood perceived differently from the same person in a confident mood.

Other subjective factors are more largely due to environmental causes, to the effects of training, to the establishment of particular interests, to the persistence of special attitudes, to the effects of experience, familiarity and the like. When, for example, the ordinary person is reading a book, he does not read letter by letter, or even word by word. Experiments have shown [2] that his eye travels over the lines in a series of jerks, making only one or two brief halts on the way. This indicates that during the few moments at which his eye is at rest he is perceiving several words together. What he does, in fact, is to gain the meaning of the sentence by perceiving some part of the outlines of the words, and filling in the rest by inference—a process that will be illustrated more fully in a later portion of this chapter. He is able to perceive the words from their outlines by reason of his familiarity with those outlines. This is one reason why sensible words are so much more easily perceived than nonsense words. Nonsense words have unfamiliar outlines, and the greater the familiarity of the words and of their setting the easier is it for the processes of inference leading to perception (and to recognition) to occur.[3] In some cases, however, a thing may stand out

[1] Bartlett (2).   [2] See, for example, Vernon (9).
[3] See, for example, Koffka (3), p. 569.

because of its *unfamiliarity*, but in these cases the perception will not depend on inference.

Now, when the ordinary person tries to correct proofs he finds it very difficult. In proof-reading an entirely different approach must be adopted, each letter must be considered separately to see if it is turned, out of line, worn, from the wrong fount or case, to see if the spacing and the punctuation are correct, and so on. But trained proof-readers do all this with comparative ease. They have learnt by experience and by training how to do it, and how to alter their attitude and mental " set " according to whether they are reading normally or reading proofs.

The establishment of mental sets depends to a large extent on our interests, both permanent and transitory, and many of these are the result of our experience and training. Most books on psychology relate how if individuals with different interests— for example a geologist, a botanist and an artist—go on a country walk together, the description of their walk which each may give on his return may be so different as hardly to be recognisable as descriptions of the same walk.

BARTLETT'S EXPERIMENTS

The effect of mental sets, of inferences and of working on reduced cues was brought out in Bartlett's experiments.[1] Here the observers drew on paper what they thought they had just had exposed to them. The exposures were short, and there was often insufficient time for all the details to be observed. Fig. 1 shows examples of some of the objects that were exposed in the first series of experiments. In this series it was found that *names* were often used in the descriptions. Thus (1) was often called a square with one of its sides gone, (2) was said to be a " Z " upside down, (3) was called an " N ", though it was correctly reproduced by everybody, and (4) was called a square with diagonals. In this case the gap was almost always noticed and reproduced, but its position was often wrong.

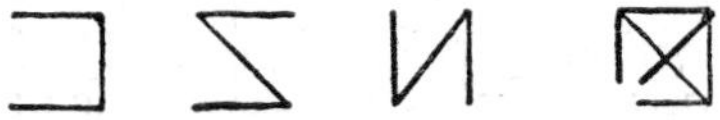

FIG. 1.

Names were usually given as soon as the designs had been exhibited, and then the observer felt more satisfied. In these cases the names did not affect the accuracy of the representation,

[1] Bartlett (2).

though there were other cases in which they did. This was seen in the second series that Bartlett gave his observers. Examples are given in Fig. 2. While some of these were intended to be representational, others were intended to be meaningless. Each design in the series was re-acted to as a single unit, but the observers hesitated a little longer than in the first series before putting down what they had seen. Naming occupied a position of great

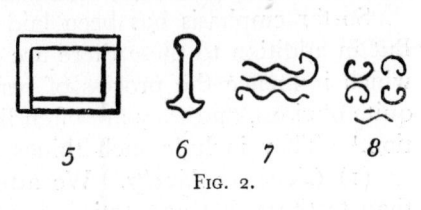

FIG. 2.

importance in this series, for it often influenced the reproduction. Thus (6) was once called a pick-axe and represented with pointed prongs ; once it was termed a turf-cutter and made with a rounded blade ; it was called in part a key (the handle) and in part a shovel (the blade) and changed accordingly. Six observers called it an anchor and increased the size of the ring at the top. Again, (5) was twice called a picture frame, the representations being shown in Fig. 3. But the observer who spoke of it as two carpenter's squares placed together reproduced it correctly.

(7) and (8) were always attacked by analogy. The analogy had nearly always to do with the shape of the figure or with the disposition of its lines or curves. Sometimes there was a tendency to multiply detail. This was first noticed with (7) but became more pronounced later on.

One complicated design showed a closed gate, a brick wall and a notice board. Although the letters on the notice board were too small and the length of exposure too short for the observers to be able to read what was written on it, yet 80 per cent. of them said it was " Trespassers will be prosecuted ", thus indicating the influence of inference.

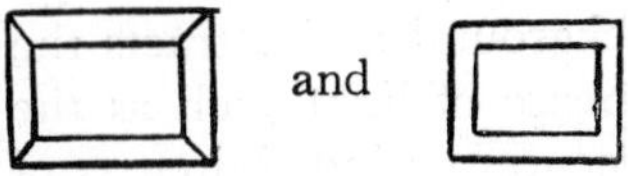

Generally speaking, what was found in these experiments was that certain dominant details stood out. With the simple material

and

FIG. 3.

this would be gaps, and odd and disconnected material ; with the complex material it might be the plan of construction, if any, or its general topic and representational significance. The dominant details (which might be different for different individuals) were the important things and acted as a kind of

c

nucleus about which the rest of the details—often inferred, and sometimes wrongly inferred—clustered.

FACTORS IN ATTENTION

So far emphasis has been laid chiefly on subjective factors. But in addition to these there are a number of objective factors which influence the process of perception. Many of these are quite obvious, and they are often listed as determinants of attention.[1] They include such things as the following :

(1) *Change or Novelty.* We attend to moving objects rather than to those that are stationary : we do not notice the ticking of a familiar clock until it alters its character in some way, e.g. by stopping : we ignore the pressure of our clothes on our bodies and the pressure of our bodies on the soles of our feet unless an unexpected change, like walking over broken or uneven ground, occurs.

(2) *Strength.* A strong stimulus is more likely to attract attention than a weak one, unless the weak stimulus on account of its weakness possesses some striking quality.

(3) *Size.* Tall people are more noticeable than short as a rule, unless the divergence from the normal is very marked. In such a case the extremes at both ends are easily noticed, e.g. a dwarf is almost as noticeable as a giant.

(4) *Striking Quality.* It is stated that high notes are more *arresting* than low ; that itch, tickle and pain gain attention in preference to a broad, smooth touch ; and that saturated colours, though having less intensity of light than pale colours, are stronger stimuli for attention.

(5) *Repetition.* The repetition of a stimulus increases the likelihood that it will attract attention, provided that the repetition is not so frequent that fatigue or adaptation occurs.

(6) *Definite Form.* A sharply defined object, even though smaller in size, stands out from its background and attracts the eye more than a broad, indefinite expanse of light such as the sky. This is true unless the very vagueness or indefiniteness of the object's form gives it some unusual and therefore striking quality.

(7) Other factors are *aptness* and *recency*, both of which are made use of to a large extent by advertisers.

[1] See, for example, Woodworth (10), p. 45.

Objective Factors in Perceiving

Apart from these factors there are, as the work of the Gestalt psychologists [1] in particular has shown, certain other features concerning the structure of the objects themselves which influence their organisation and the way they are perceived.

(a) *Grouping.* In any perceptual situation certain things are grouped together and differentiated from others. This is one of the difficulties of performing experiments on the "span of apprehension" and the "span of attention". If it is desired to know how many objects an individual can correctly perceive at a single glance, the simplest thing to do would appear to be to present him with a series of cards in an irregular order on which are drawn a different number of objects, and to note the largest number of objects he can perceive correctly.

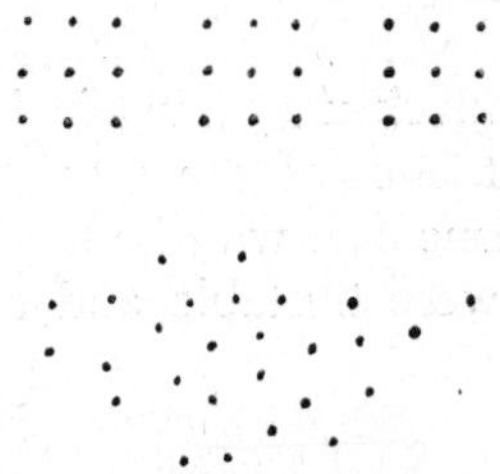

Fig. 4.

A refinement of this procedure is a commonplace of experimental psychology. But when experiments of this kind are done it is found that one of the difficulties is to arrange the objects on the cards in such a way that they do not form groups. It is much easier to estimate the number of objects when they can be grouped together than when they are perceived as discrete objects without any interconnection. It is, for example, much easier to perceive the first arrangement of dots in Fig. 4 as twenty-seven than it is to perceive the second arrangement as the same number. This tendency towards grouping appears in almost every case : even the second group will tend to form itself into a few groups of a few dots each if it is looked at for a sufficient length of time.

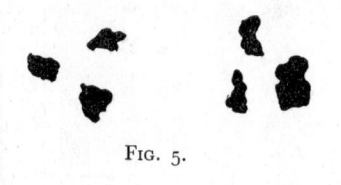

Fig. 5.

(b) *Nearness.* Grouping was also brought out in Köhler's [2] example illustrated in Fig. 5. This is seen as two groups of three blots each, not as three groups of two nor as six separate patches. In this particular case it is probable that the relative nearness of some of the patches to one another, compared with their distance from others, causes this organisation to occur.

[1] See, for example, Köhler (4), Chaps. 5 and 6 ; Koffka (3), Chaps. 4 and 5.
[2] Köhler (4), p. 118.

(c) *Similarity.* In Fig. 6 the dots are nearer to the circles than they are to one another, and yet the first pattern tends to be seen as horizontal rows rather than as vertical columns, while the second tends to be seen as vertical columns rather than as horizontal rows.

(d) *Symmetry.* Bahnsen[1] exposed the designs shown in Fig. 7 to 64 people. The first can be seen as black symmetrical or white unsymmetrical stripes; the second as white symmetrical or black unsymmetrical stripes. He found that in 89 per cent. of the cases the symmetrical stripes were reported, and in only one case was the unsymmetrical form reported. The other cases were unstable and ambiguous.

FIG. 6.

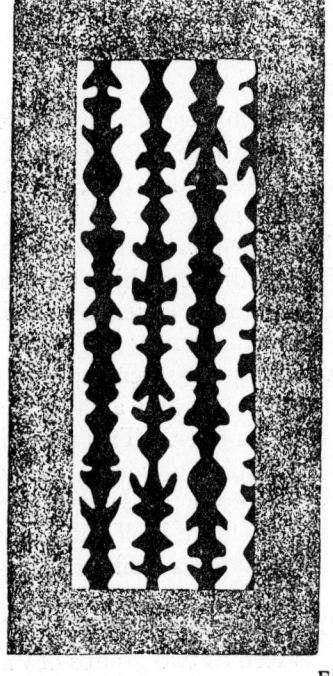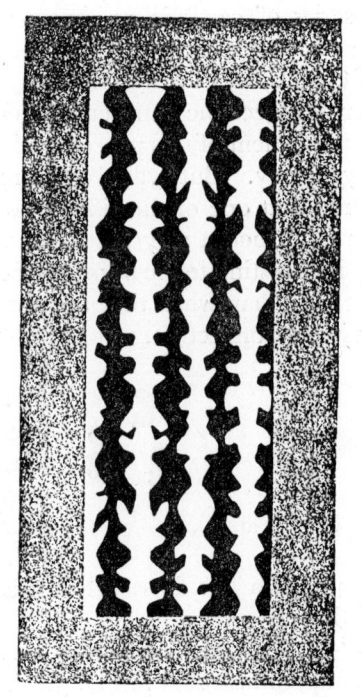

FIG. 7.

(e) *Closure.* The six equidistant lines in the first diagram of Fig. 8 tend at first sight to be seen as six discrete units. There is no immediate tendency to rearrange them in groups in any

[1] Bahnsen (1).

special way. If, however, a small horizontal line is added at the top and bottom of each, the result is quite different, and, as can be seen in the second diagram, they at once form themselves into three discrete figures composed of two vertical lines each. The effect of the small horizontal lines is to make one see closed figures, and the effect is such that whereas the lines *a, b, c, d, e,* and *f* formerly looked equidistant, yet now the line *b* appears to be nearer to *a* than to *c*, and similarly with the remaining lines.

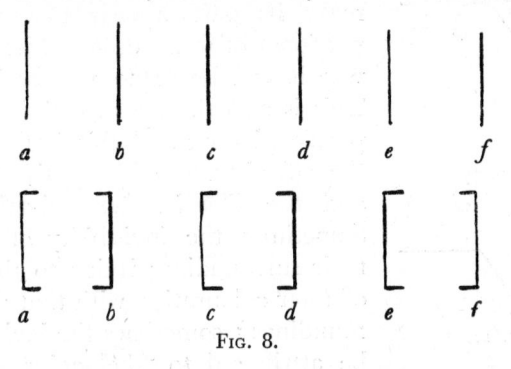

FIG. 8.

(*f*) *Good Continuation*. The factor of closure is closely related to another factor called by the Gestalt psychologists " good continuation ". This may be illustrated by Köhler's [1] " figure 4 " diagram illustrated in Fig. 9.   Between the two big figures in the diagram there is a figure 4. It is difficult to see it because the two vertical strokes form part of the two big figures, and the

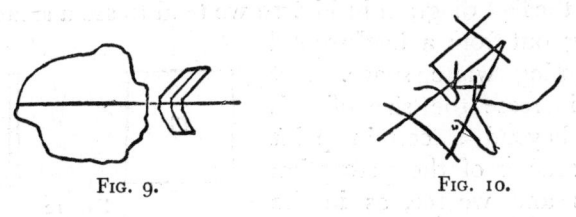

FIG. 9.   FIG. 10.

horizontal stroke forms a part of the long horizontal line. Thus each part of the figure 4 is an essential part of another pattern, each part continues a pattern or closes a figure and consequently the unity of the figure 4 itself is destroyed. It is not merely that we do not see the figure 4 because the whole diagram is unfamiliar, and that it is therefore in an unfamiliar setting, for quite as unfamiliar a setting can be arranged, as is shown in Fig. 10, in which the figure 4 stands out clearly.

[1] Köhler (4), p. 155.

Many other examples of good continuation can be given. It is, for example, easier to see Fig. 11 as being composed of a straight line and an " S " curve than as being composed of the crook and hook figures illustrated underneath it. The crook on the right appears to be an essential part of the curve on the left, it forms a unity with it, and it loses its continuation with the straight line. This is the art of camouflage : first to break up the unity of a particular object and then to make its parts appear to form essential portions of some other object. In that way it can be made to lose its identity. This is also the art of the devizer of the puzzle picture, and this is the reason for the effectiveness of protective colouration and the like in the animal kingdom. Sometimes the invisibility of animals in their surroundings is due to the similarity of their colouration with that of their surroundings : sometimes the invisibility may be attributed to " belongingness " rather than to similarity, the animal becoming assimilated into the background owing to its apparently forming an essential part of it.

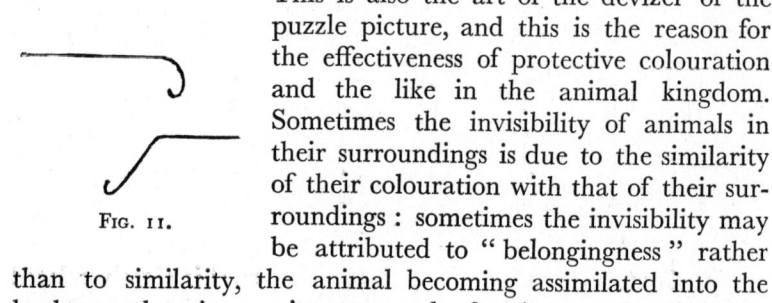

Fig. 11.

(g) *The Figure-ground Phenomenon.* This leads us to a consideration of what is known as the " figure-ground " Phenomenon, which plays an important part in normal perceiving. If we look at the first diagram in Fig. 12 we tend to see a small square standing out from a background of enclosing white space. But if we increase the size of this square beyond a certain point the character of the perception changes and we see, as in the second diagram, a double square standing out as the figure with the enclosed white space as background. The enclosed white space from being figure has changed to background. When this occurs the enclosed white space, which previously appeared to stand out from the background, now appears as if it lay behind the double square. And this is what happens in general. The figure appears to stand out from the background ; the background appears to lie behind the figure.

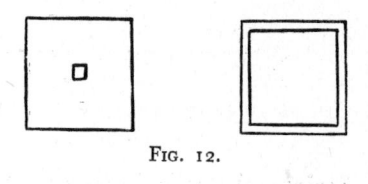

Fig. 12.

Synæsthesia

Turning from these factors of normal perceiving let us consider some of the features of perceiving in rather more unusual forms. Sometimes a perception is interpreted in terms of a different sense organ from the one that is stimulated, and in some of such cases it is called " synæsthesia ". A similar phenomenon occurs quite frequently in normal perception. Thus if we listen to the sound of aeroplanes passing overhead we may think of the aeroplanes themselves rather than of the sound. Or we may look out of the window and see that it is wet, though wetness is really something that is felt rather than something which can be seen. In these cases we can readily explain our interpretation in a different sense organ from that which is stimulated in terms of experiences which are common to a great number of people.[1] But in other cases the connections are obscure and uncommon (even though they may be constant for any given individual) and in these cases we talk of synæsthesias.

The commonest type of synæsthesia is that in which a sound gives rise to a perception of a clear, or even a vivid, colour. It is not merely that the sound reminds the person of a colour, nor that it seems to be like a colour, but that it is really seen as a colour. A number of such cases have been investigated. In one of them [2] the colours seen ranged from dark brown, which was perceived when low tones were sounded, through brown which accompanied middle C, through pink to dark blue, and then to light blue, and finally through green to grey at the maximum upper range of hearing.

Now just as normal perceptions in terms of sense organs different from those stimulated can be interpreted through common past experiences, so it is likely that synæsthesias may be partly explicable in terms of individual experiences. This view has been criticised by some authorities who believe that synæsthesia has an hereditary basis, and they point to cases of synæsthesia arising in individuals in whom there is no traceable past experience to account for their development. However, there is at present practically no evidence to indicate the type of hereditary mechanism at work, or the way in which the phenomenon is inherited. Myers, in fact, showed that when " coloured hearing " did occur in more than one member of the same family there was disagreement among them about the colour to be

[1] See, for example, Morgan (5), Chap. 3.   [2] Myers (6).

attached to any given tone. It has to be remembered also that some associations between different sense organs may be built up without a person being fully aware of the fact, and without consciously connecting the two together. Nevertheless, until more evidence has been produced we must regard the phenomenon of synæsthesia as without an adequate explanation at the present time.

ILLUSIONS

An *illusion* is an inaccurate perception of a sense impression. Many illusions, particularly those in the visual field, are of common experience and shared by almost everybody. One of these is the Müller-Lyer illusion illustrated in Fig. 13. Here the distance from *A* to *B* appears to be considerably shorter than the distance from *C* to *D*, although they are in fact the same.

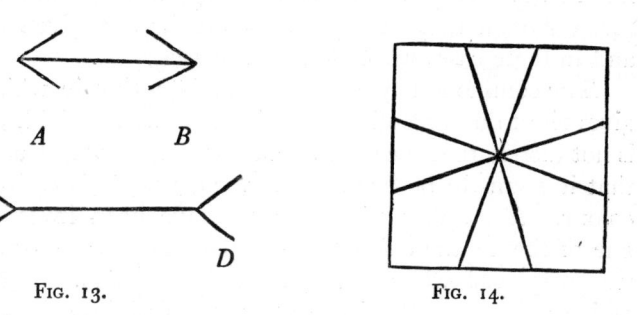

FIG. 13.   FIG. 14.

Part of this illusion is perhaps due to the methods of perceiving which we have built up as a result of our experience, for it is interesting to notice that Rivers [1] found that the illusion was far less pronounced among the Torres Straits inhabitants than it is among ourselves. Nevertheless there is little doubt that in this and in others of a similar type the main determining factor is not the result of individual idiosyncrasy. Sometimes, however, illusions are more individual and depend on a person's own interests, or on the line along which his attitude happens to be directed. The latter is particularly noticeable in ambiguous figures, e.g. the Maltese cross-propeller figure illustrated in Fig. 14, where the object perceived may depend in part on the direction of the individual's attention before the figure is presented, or on the instructions that are given to him before

[1] Rivers (7), p. 125.

the presentation is made. Expectation or anticipation or anxiety is important, too, in the common illusions of ordinary life, e.g. when a person left alone in a house at night interprets any sounds as a burglar or attacker.

How, then, may the accuracy of a perception be determined ? One way, which frequently does not carry much conviction, and which in any case may be misleading, is to appeal to other people. This will obviously only be of any use if our illusion is an individual, and not a general, illusion. It would be of no use to appeal to social judgment over the Müller-Lyer illusion, for other people will be as subject to the illusion as we are ourselves. Even in other cases, however, social judgment has sometimes proved to be wrong. This, therefore, is the weakest test we can apply. A much stronger test is to appeal to experiment, e.g. by applying a ruler to the Müller-Lyer illusion one can prove that the distance between A and B is no less than that between C and D. This will be enough to convince us that we are suffering from an illusion. In the third place, however, it is sometimes possible to check the illusion by appealing to other senses. Sometimes, because of emotional factors, this is not easy to carry out in practice. It is not easy, for example, if we see a shadow lurking in the woods at night to go boldly up to the wood to investigate the shadow by touch. Nor is it easy to get out of bed to investigate whether the sound we heard was in fact a burglar. But in other cases this may be done, as when, taken in by the waxwork policeman or programme seller at Madame Tussaud's, we convince ourselves of our illusion by touch : or when, taken in by the illusion that there is water on the road when we are driving a car on a sunny day, we convince ourselves of our mistake either by the experiment of driving through the apparently wet patch of road only to find there is no splashing, or by getting out of the car and feeling the road surface.

It would only be very unusual people who would need to apply this last test, and for some of them even this test would not prove convincing. They would be people who had some strong emotional background to the illusion, who wanted to believe it was true, and who were prepared to go on believing it to be true in spite of any evidence to the contrary. This type of continuing false perception, which may even in some cases occur without *any* external impression at all, leads us to the question of *hallucinations*.

HALLUCINATIONS

It is difficult to draw a fine distinction between illusions and hallucinations. Some authorities have done so on the grounds that in an illusion there is an external object which is wrongly perceived, but that in an hallucination there is no external object, and the stimulus giving rise to the hallucination arises within the cortex itself. But other authorities believe that it is sometimes proper to refer to a person as suffering from an hallucination even though it is impossible to be certain that no external object is giving rise to his condition.

Hallucinations, as a rule, are far more subject to individual interpretation than are illusions, although cases are on record—particularly when the people suffering them are under the influence of drugs or in an advanced state of alcoholism—in which the same kind of hallucination seems to occur in many different people. Then, too, there is usually a much stronger emotional interest in the hallucination than there is in the illusion, in many of which, e.g. the Müller-Lyer illusion, there is merely a mild degree of interest or amusement. Furthermore, the hallucination is usually so real to the person seeing it that he continues to believe in it even after its existence has been proved to him to be impossible. This degree of belief in the existence of the hallucination forms a link between it and the *delusion* which we shall consider in the next chapter.

Auditory hallucinations are perhaps the commonest, and they are encountered very frequently in mental-hospital patients. Sometimes they consist merely of a continuous buzzing or ringing in the ears : sometimes they consist of " voices " which tell the person to do this or not to do that : sometimes the voices do not speak directly to the patient, but make remarks about him, occasionally using the most obscene language which shocks the patient to the core.

Visual hallucinations are the next commonest. Sometimes they take the form of continuous flashes of light or coloured rainbows : sometimes they are more elaborate and consist, let us say, of a man with an evil face and a long nose working away hour after hour at a grindstone. Hallucinations of taste and smell, of pain and of kinæsthesis are also encountered. The last sometimes take the form of levitation, in which the patient feels that he is being moved from place to place, although in fact no movement has occurred. Perhaps the levitation that occurs in

spiritualistic séances is of this type, and it may, in such cases, be illusory rather than hallucinatory—due to vaguely perceived movement in the dimly-lit room which gives the person the feeling that he himself is moving rather than the other object, in much the same way as we get the impression of movement when we sit in a stationary train and watch another train move past.

Hallucinations occur more frequently when a person is very tired than when he is fresh. A person who is unaccustomed to it who spends a whole day typing may get a visual and kinæsthetic hallucination of typing afterwards. Or, after spending a day in a boat on the river, he may continue to feel the rocking movement. Or, after spending a day at Niagara Falls, he may continue to hear the sound of the falling water when he is in bed that night 50 miles away.

A person is more likely, too, to have hallucinations as a result of taking some drug. The hallucinations of the advanced alcoholic have already been mentioned, and they are well known to be an indication that the person has indulged too much. Other drugs often provide hallucinatory experiences. Under the influence of *mescalin* intoxication, for example, I myself saw what appeared to be drops of sap running continuously along the furrows of the table at which I was sitting. The table, too, seemed to be semitransparent, and *The Times* which was lying on the table seemed to bend upwards and downwards as if it were breathing. At a later stage of intoxication I saw intricate patterns in vivid colours projected on the wall. The patterns were in a constant state of flux and were continually changing both in form and in colour. Such hallucinations are also said to be characteristic of hashish intoxication. Again, cocaine is reported to give tactual hallucinations, patients complaining that small creatures and parasites are crawling over or beneath their skin.

Hallucinations may also be produced under hypnosis, and the most startling effects may sometimes be secured in this way. Apart from such minor things as getting the patient to read an imaginary book and turn over the pages appropriately, more violent reactions may be obtained by tipping an envelope of imaginary fleas down his neck, or telling him that some particular member of the audience is his baby who needs a bath.

Again, too, hallucinations may occur as the result of some strong emotion, particularly when they can act in that way as a defence mechanism. Here, as with other hallucinations, the

patient firmly believes in the truth of his hallucinations. And once more we encounter the difficulty of making a clear distinction between hallucinations and delusions.

REFERENCES

1. BAHNSEN, P., " Eine Untersuchung über Symmetrie und Asymmetrie bei visuellen Wahrnehmungen ". *Zeitschr. f. Psychol.*, 1928, **108**, 129–54.
2. BARTLETT, F. C., *Remembering*. Cambridge : University Press, 1932, pp. 317.
3. KOFFKA, K., *Principles of Gestalt Psychology*. London : Kegan Paul, 1935, pp. 720.
4. KÖHLER, W., *Gestalt Psychology*. London : Bell, 1930, pp. 312.
5. MORGAN, J. J. B., *The Psychology of Abnormal People*. London : Longmans, Green, 1928, pp. 627.
6. MYERS, C. S., " A Case of Synæsthesia ". *Brit. J. Psychol.*, 1911, **4**, 228–38.
7. RIVERS, W. H. R., *Reports of the Cambridge Anthropological Expedition to Torres Straits (Ed.,* A. C. Haddon). Cambridge : University Press, 1901, Vol. 2.
8. THOULESS, R. H., *General and Social Psychology*. London : University Tutorial Press, 1937, pp. 522.
9. VERNON, M. D., *The Experimental Study of Reading*. Cambridge : University Press, 1931, pp. 190.
10. WOODWORTH, R. S., *Psychology*. London : Methuen, 12th edn., 1940, pp. 632.

CHAPTER III

BELIEF, DELUSIONS AND THINKING

DETERMINANTS OF BELIEF

The difficulty of distinguishing between some hallucinations and delusions leads us to the question of belief and the general conditions which help to determine the development of beliefs. It has sometimes been stated, and more often been held, that the beliefs of our own culture are built on a system of logical coherence and consistency. Those which are inconsistent with the body of accepted facts which we have built up through our own experience, and which we have been led by our education to accept as established by the work of philosophers and scientists, we tend to regard as untrue. New beliefs which we can test by direct perception, by the use of instruments, by the processes of logical inference, or by reference to a scientist or philosopher of established reputation, and which we find to be consistent with our accepted body of beliefs, we tend to accept as true. Occasionally, however, a discovery may be made which, if true, would oblige us to revise many of the fundamental beliefs we already hold. In such cases we are only prepared to accept the new discovery, with all its implications, after its validity has been established beyond question by a number of independent workers, and after its truth has been accepted by individuals who are specially qualified to pronounce a verdict on the question.

This, at any rate, is how we like to think our beliefs are built up. In actual fact, however, this coldly analytical approach is rarely achieved in practice.[1] Even if we begin by being faced with a problem, coming to some conclusion, putting that conclusion to the test to verify it and finding that it is true, we will have difficulty in dealing with a similar kind of problem on a subsequent occasion with the same air of meritorious detachment. Perhaps in some respects it is a good thing that we do, for if we were obliged to withhold judgment on every new problem, however unimportant, until it had been verified, or until it had been shown to be untrue, it is probable that there would be few things on which we would consider a decision to be justified, and our daily life would be mainly spent in vacillation, uncertainty

---

[1] See, for example, Thouless (12).

and lack of action.   In fact what happens is that when a new problem is put to the test and found to be true we experience an emotion of satisfaction which tends to impress on our memory that type of solution, so that if a somewhat similar problem is encountered later on, we tend to turn first of all to the type of solution which was found to be correct in the parallel problem earlier on.   That type of solution is much easier for us to accept than any other.   Here is the introduction of subjective conditions.   We tend to believe what we want to believe, or what gave us satisfaction before.[1]

The social influences, or the beliefs of the group to which we belong are also of considerable importance.   Many examples may be quoted of beliefs which are held among the simpler peoples which we do not accept, not merely because they conflict with our established beliefs, but because they are not currently believed in our community.   For instance, it is reported that some of the Kaffirs when hunting tell the animal they are hunting to come out from the forest because they are not looking for it but for some other animal ; or that there is a tribe in New Guinea the members of which read out a letter to a tree before cutting it down.   The letter informs the tree that the Dutch government has ordered it to be cut down and that the tribe itself is therefore blameless.

Similarly, too, with magic and omens and spells.   If you make a wax model of a person and destroy it by sticking pins into it or by putting it into the fire, may you not perhaps bring some evil influence to bear on the person himself ?   Or if you secure some parings of a person's nails and destroy them may you not perhaps do him some damage, for the nail parings once formed a part of his person ?   Or if it is possible to transfer warmth from one person to another, may it not be possible to transfer other things, such as courage or sexual potency or fear, as well ?   Therefore it is desirable to wear the clothes of warriors, it is undesirable to eat the flesh of hares : in the one case you may assimilate some of the warrior's courage ; in the other you may assimilate some of the hare's timidity.

Magic and omens and spells are types of faulty generalisation which are supported and made more acceptable by strong emotional factors.   We see in them the extent to which belief

---

[1] Though it is true that in exceptional conditions, e.g. in moods of pessimism or old age or in certain weather conditions, we sometimes tend to believe what we want *not* to believe.

may depend on emotional factors. Now although it may appear to us as rather peculiar that people are willing to believe such things, yet we ourselves, in spite of the benefits of a scientific education, often in our " normal " behaviour show the influence of emotional factors. In spite of scientific education many people, even if they do not actually believe in superstitions, yet have a feeling of *malaise* about them. Spilt salt, broken mirrors, walking under ladders and many others are still avoided for emotional reasons, even if a person is prepared to agree that there is no intellectual justification for the beliefs. These beliefs are of common occurrence ; but other false beliefs are less common. Both types, however, conform to the description which some authorities have given of pathological delusions, namely that (1) they are not true to facts, (2) they are not subject to correction by appeal to reason, and (3) they are out of harmony with the individual's education and environment.

DETERMINANTS OF DELUSIONS

The cultural pattern of some societies makes it a commonplace for most of the members of that society to hold beliefs that we would regard as delusional. For instance, Benedict [1] describes the Dobuans as living in an atmosphere laden with suspicion. No woman leaves her cooking a moment untended for fear that someone will gain access to it and poison the food. The Dobuan thinks that every moment of prosperity has to be wrung from a malicious world, and that all existence is a cut-throat struggle in which quarter is neither asked nor given. Suspicion and cruelty are his weapons, and virtue consists in selecting a victim on whom he can vent his malignancy. He lives out without repression man's worst nightmares of the ill-will of the universe.

Anyone holding beliefs of this kind in our society would be lucky to escape confinement in an institution, yet it is the typical pattern of belief in Dobuan society. It is remarkable how greatly the current attitudes in a community can influence the beliefs of the majority of its members. In our own society, with its attempts to apply intellectual criteria, some errors of belief are undoubtedly due to errors of judgment. In so far as this is true they may be corrected as the individual who holds them encounters different experiences which indicate to him his errors. And such revisions and corrections are continually being made.

---

[1] Benedict (1). Chap. 5.

But other errors of belief depend on emotional rather than on intellectual factors, and these cannot be influenced by intellectual means. It is easy to understand how many of them arise. To be in a condition of doubt is always unpleasant, for in such circumstances we are under stress and tension. If our minds are not made up relevant action will be impossible. The acceptance of a belief brings relief : then, at any rate, we can get on with the job. It is easy to see, therefore, why so many beliefs, even false beliefs, are so strongly held. We resist the possibility that we may be wrong, for to accept this possibility will throw us into uncertainty and inaction again. It is so much easier to accept the current nostrum : to attribute any misfortune to " the government " or " the Jews " or to the fact that we planted our spring cabbages when the moon was full, or to leave any important decision to be decided not by the efforts of our own powers of reasoning but by the way in which a tossed coin may fall. In all such cases, too, we have the support of a body of opinion within our own community and we can excuse, even if we cannot justify, our decision by appealing to the verdict of other people—to the influence, that is to say, of our pattern of culture.

Sometimes, however, our beliefs are more individual : they are not shared by other people, who may in fact hold a contrary view. Then, assuming that the belief is based on emotional rather than on rational grounds, it will not be possible to alter it by an appeal to reason. What usually happens in such cases is that more and more reasons are found why the belief must be true, each one countering the reason that is put forward why it must be false. If, for example, we are really afraid that our actions are guided too much by selfish ends, ends that we do not like admitting to ourselves, we often try to find more acceptable and more noble reasons for them. Similarly, too, a person with a delusion is someone who wants to believe a certain thing that is false. He has to believe it or his mental peace will be disturbed. But he cannot admit this even to himself and still less to other people. So he tries to make the belief appear rational, and he seeks for reasons why it must be true. In this way he often succeeds in diverting his own attention and that of other people from the real motive for his belief on to a consideration of the validity of his arguments, and if he succeeds in doing this he can remain undisturbed by the effort of making an emotional readjustment. Many delusions can be cured only if the individual

who holds them can be made to want to believe something else. Reasoning will never make him change them.

Delusions reach perhaps the greatest degree of complexity in the systematised beliefs of paranoid schizophrenics.[1] The number of reasons which the paranoid patient is prepared to put forward why the unusual collection of reputable and respectable people are plotting to encompass his downfall is really astonishing. Delusions are also a feature of other types of schizophrenia and of other pathological syndromes. By way of illustrating some of the mental processes I may perhaps mention my own delusions under the influence of *mescalin*. Two or three hours after I had had the injection I became extremely self-centred. I considered my condition to be the most important thing that had ever happened, and I thought that all the doctors in the hospital where I was working at the time would inevitably be of the same opinion, and would be discussing me and my symptoms all the time. But I was also apt to take offence on the slightest provocation, and any remark or action by other people which did not definitely flatter me I regarded as a form of insult. When I sat down to lunch and one of the doctors fetched me my napkin I was duly flattered, but when somebody else, remarking on my condition, said how nice it must be to feel oneself the centre of the universe I was gravely offended. Any telephone call that came through to the luncheon room for one or other of the doctors I was quite convinced must be from the medical superintendent wishing to interview me, and I imagined that all the other doctors must be talking about me and my symptoms as their sole topic of conversation. In particular, I noticed one of the doctors sitting on the window-sill conversing with another who was sitting at one of the tables. I was sure they were talking about me and glancing in my direction. So I suddenly looked up to verify my impression, only to find that they were not looking in my direction after all. My immediate reaction was to think how clever they had been to look away in time, so that I should not catch them looking at me. When it was time for me to leave the table I had the greatest possible reluctance to going alone because I felt that everybody would be looking at me as I went. On the other hand I knew that if I asked anyone to accompany me it would be likely to give rise to discussion after I had gone. In fact I did ask one of the doctors

---

[1] Curran and Guttmann (2), pp. 105–6 ; Mapother and Lewis (7), pp. 1868–9 ; Fisher (4), pp. 299–301, 333–4.

at my table to accompany me, thus taking the line of action which in fact was most likely to make me conspicuous.

In delusions, therefore, one can often see a train of thought executed with logical consistency, and were the premises correct, the conclusion would follow inevitably. But in delusions the premises are false, they cannot be corrected by an appeal to reason, and they are out of harmony with a person's education and environment. It is true that I knew before I took the *mescalin* the kind of hallucinations and delusions that I might experience. It is true also that for a large part of the time I knew that what I was experiencing was the result of having taken the drug. But this did not prevent me from believing that what I was experiencing was any the less true. The same thing is sometimes found in well-preserved and intelligent schizophrenics soon after their delusions have arisen. They may agree with you that their beliefs are absurd, but they will pathetically confess that they cannot help feeling that they are true all the same. This does not often occur, but occasionally it does. The more usual thing is for the schizophrenic to have no real insight into the possibility that his beliefs may be false. I lost my own insight about tea-time on the day I had taken *mescalin*. Somebody suggested playing a game of tennis and I said I would like to make up a four. But then when somebody else remembered I had taken *mescalin*, came over to take my pulse and recommended me not to play, I began to think that I was really very ill and that I might collapse at any moment. And later when the doctor who had given me the drug looked into the room where I was sitting just before going home, asked me where I lived and said he had to go in that direction himself, I interpreted this to mean that he thought I was too ill to go alone. He said he would be ready in five minutes, and this served to reinforce my belief, for I thought that he must have noticed how ill I looked, that I really was not fit to go just then, and that he was trying tactfully to give me the impression that there was still something he wanted to do in the hospital. And when we eventually left the hospital and crossed the street to catch a bus, I saw that there was one drawn up at the stopping-place. I waited to see if my companion would make any attempt to hurry to catch it, and when he did not I thought he had purposely refrained because he did not want me to over-exert myself. During this stage of my hypochondriacal delusion I fully and entirely believed I was very ill physically, and I had not the smallest glimmer of insight.

MENTAL PROCESSES IN THINKING

If, then, some delusions carry through thought processes logically, although they are based on false premises, let us consider the processes of thinking when the premises are not so untrue. Those who have analysed the mental processes involved in the solution of problems trace the following succession of processes as one passes towards the solution.[1] There is often first of all a feeling of discomfort, followed by an attempt to locate the difficulty in order to see what has to be done : sometimes the location of the difficulty will be incorrect. The next stage is usually the emergence of some suggestion about how the problem can be solved : often such suggestions suddenly spring into consciousness, apparently from nowhere, and without a preceding intellectual preparation for them. If the suggestion is obviously satisfactory it will be accepted at once ; if it is obviously absurd it will be at once rejected, often without any intervening mental processes which can be reported. The suggestions which occur usually show similarities with the methods which have in the past been found to be successful in solving similar problems. Then the intellectual aspect of the matter may appear, the suggestion may be elaborated and its implications worked out more fully before it is either rejected or accepted. But at this stage the solution may be delayed from one of two opposing tendencies. Either a suggestion may be dropped before it has been sufficiently elaborated, or it may be persisted in and its implications further and further elaborated after it ought to have become obvious that it is in fact a fruitless line of elaboration. If the suggestion is finally accepted as providing a solution to the problem, pleasurable feeling tone will be experienced : this is especially true if the problem is one that the individual has found interesting and difficult. Correspondingly, if the suggestion is finally rejected, this will be accompanied by unpleasurable feeling tone, especially if the suggestion has been elaborated at length. If the suggestion is rejected and the individual persists in trying to solve the problem, there will be a return to the stage of the emergence of another suggestion. If he is not interested in the problem, or if he feels lazy, or if he feels the problem is too difficult, a number of irrelevant thoughts are likely to emerge during the course of his thinking, and the nature of these irrelevant thoughts may be determined by his interests, either without reference to the prob-

[1] Cp. Dewey (3).

lem, or else, more often, by something in the problem associated with a personal interest. This is the experience of being side-tracked. In all cases, however, a solution or an attempt at a solution by reasoning involves some kind of novel combination of familiar material. In all cases the material with which we are dealing has to be rearranged and reformulated before the solution to the problem will appear.

Varying Degrees of Control over the Processes of Association

Most of the characteristics we have just considered occur when a person's mental processes are subjected to the most complete control that it is possible for him to exercise. Many of his other mental processes are not so strictly subjected to control.[1] Perhaps the smallest degree of control is exercised in what is sometimes called *free association* and sometimes called *reverie*. Here one lets one's mind wander from one topic to another without conscious direction or control, and finds, when one eventually stops to think about the mental processes that have taken place, that one has finished a very long way from one's starting-point, and that the connections between one topic and the next are very slight.

In *dreaming* there is usually a slightly greater degree of control over the direction of the associations. Even though there is still much apparent illogicality in the sequences, yet usually there is some connecting thread which one can disentangle.

In *phantasy* or *day-dreaming* there is still greater control over the direction of the associations. The wish-fulfilment motive, which many analysts believe to be the main determinant of dreams, is more obvious to the conscious mind in phantasy. Usually the phantasy is of the " conquering hero " type. Even in the " suffering martyr " phantasy—a type which is not uncommon— the principal is usually redeemed in the end, with the praise and honour he so richly deserves over-generously provided by the very same people who have so cruelly misunderstood and mal-treated him in the past, and who are now doing their best to salve some portion of their guilty consciences.

From free association, through dreaming, through phantasy to controlled thinking we see a progression from little or no conscious control over the processes of association up to the greatest degree of control of which the individual is capable.

[1] Morgan (8), Chap. 4.

But even in thinking the amount of direction and control which may be exercised varies very much from one person to another, and also within the same person at different times.

In the first place we may consider the various ways in which an individual's control over his thinking may be limited by an actual poverty of associations.

(1) *Education.* A person who suffers from the results of a poor education or no education at all will clearly be at a disadvantage both in the number and in the richness of his associations compared with one who has been more fortunate in this respect. Different types of education and experience will also largely determine the direction along which the richness of associations may develop. Thus, for example, a country child will appear to have a poverty of associations compared with a town child when the subject in question concerns something typically urban ; and the town child will appear at as much of a disadvantage to the country child when the topic concerns something typically rural.

(2) *Amentia.* This is a relative poverty of innate mental ability, and a person of this kind will be unable to develop his ideas and thought processes with the same degree of complexity as will a person whose innate ability is greater.

(3) *Dementia.* Here the person may at one time have possessed a reasonable degree of ability, but through some organic cause, such as syphilitic infection or senility or alcoholism now possesses mental powers which are considerably inferior to what they were in the past, with the result that his processes of thinking have suffered accordingly.

(4) *Over-specialisation.* Although a person of this type possesses a wealth of associations on the topics along which his interests have been concentrated and developed, yet outside this range he may be as ignorant and as helpless as an uneducated child or an ament.

These are some of the main causes of poverty of associations with a consequent handicap to the processes of thinking. It is hardly necessary to add, however, that other causes such as an emotional complex, inhibition, seclusiveness or emotional depression may make a person reticent and uncommunicative, and that it is therefore not always correct to infer that such a person suffers from a dearth of associations.

In the second place there may be a disturbance in the fluency of associations. This again may take several forms.

(1) *Retardation.* This is characteristic of patients suffering from depression, and it occurs also as a concomitant of some other mental maladjustments. Typically it betrays itself in the person taking an inordinate time to answer simple questions, such as giving his name or his age, and in this way it may be distinguished from the characteristic exhibited by many people who are deliberating before committing themselves to an answer. This obviously is more likely to occur with more complex problems, or ideas, though superficially such people may appear sometimes to be retarded. Occasionally patients may complain that they find it takes them a long time to answer when no retardation is apparent to the observer.

(2) *Inhibition.* In retardation a patient will give a response provided he is allowed long enough to make it, in inhibition he may or may not begin, but if he does he will stop suddenly in the middle of what he is saying and will not be coaxed any further.

(3) *Flight of Ideas.* This is a characteristic the opposite of inhibition, and it is found in some manic patients. The patient wanders from point to point with successive words and phrases connected very loosely by chance associations or by similarities of sound.

In the third place there may be a disturbance in the organisation or grouping of associations. Again this may take several forms.

(1) *Perseveration.* This sometimes occurs in organic deterioration or after a severe brain lesion, though it occurs in a less pronounced form in other cases. Typically, the patient goes on doing the same action or repeating the same phrase over and over, in spite of an attempt on his part to perform some other.

(2) *Stereotypy.* The fact of unsuccessfully trying to do or to say something else has been used to distinguish perseveration from stereotypy in which in thinking or talking the person continually reverts to the same topic.

(3) *Persistent Ideas.* These occur typically in patients who are suffering from an obsession or irrational idea, a compulsion or feeling that he must perform some action, or a phobia or irrational fear.

APHASIAS

Perhaps, however, some of the most interesting disturbances of the organisation of associations are cases of *aphasia* which

frequently occurs as the result of a brain lesion.   Head [1] classified aphasia into four main types.

(1) *Verbal Defects.*   In these the patients find great difficulty in pronouncing correctly the words they know.   In extreme cases their utterances may be reduced to only " yes " or " no ". But as speech returns their vocabulary increases, and any word they are able to recall may be used in naming an object.   At the same time the enunciation of the words remains slow and halting, and their pronunciation may be so poor that the words are hardly recognisable.   The same thing is true of their writing.   The words are very badly spelt, and the order of the letters in even very simple words cannot be remembered.   Furthermore, the power of reading to themselves for enjoyment is spoilt, for they cannot remember a series of words accurately.   That the trouble lies in the formulation of ideas is seen from the fact that when looking up the page of a book, or when scoring at cards, they may utter the wrong number and yet go on acting as if they had uttered the correct one.

(2) *Syntactical Defects.*   In this case the patients tend to talk jargon.   Not only is the utterance of individual words incorrect, but there is, in addition, a lack of grammatical coherence.   These patients can understand what they read to themselves, provided they do not have to reproduce the meaning of the words, for their internal speech is also disturbed by the tendency to talk jargon.   Sometimes they speak in a sort of baby-talk, and sometimes their speech becomes entirely unintelligible.   Unlike those suffering from verbal defects they have plenty of words : their trouble is that they cannot express them correctly.

(3) *Nominal Defects.*   This is a loss of the power to use names, and a lack of understanding of the meaning of words.   The patients fail to name objects placed in front of them, and often fail to point correctly to an object named.   They can usually count and say the alphabet, but they suffer from defective appreciation of the meaning of single numbers or letters.   Games such as cards which demand rapid and correct recognition of names and the power to register the score are impossible, though chess, draughts and dominoes may be played correctly.   Drawing from a model is easily performed, but when the patients are asked to draw from imagination the result is unsatisfactory and the distinctive parts are usually omitted.

(4) *Semantic Defects.*   These consist in a want of recognition

[1] Head (5), pp. 218-68.

of the full significance of words and phrases apart from their verbal meaning. Other functions which have nothing to do with verbalisation also suffer, for in this form of disorder there is a loss of meaning in thought. The patient's ordinary activities of daily life are usually interfered with and he is unable to do any but the simplest things. Yet in spite of this his memory and intelligence may remain on a comparatively high general level. He can remember people or events as isolated things, but if he has to describe anything or to tell a story he is liable to become confused and to omit many factors of importance. These patients tend to talk rapidly as if they are afraid of forgetting what they want to say—as in fact they often do. Thus the disorder is essentially a want of recognition of the way in which different things are related. Everything tends to be appreciated in detail and the general significance is lost. These patients therefore are unable to appreciate pictures, particularly cartoons. They can see the individual items in the cartoon correctly, but they cannot see how they are related so as to give the cartoon its point. It is often seen also in their inability to appreciate the relative value of coins, or to calculate the amount of change they ought to receive after buying something. Thus, when one of Head's patients' tobacco cost him a shilling an ounce he would ask for two ounces and place a two-shilling-piece on the counter. If he wanted a box of matches in addition he waited until the first transaction was over and then took a penny from his pocket, so as to avoid the difficulties of change. Should he happen to have nothing less than a ten-shilling note he would ask the tobacconist to give him florins only : these he counted and knew that four was the right number. But if he was given change in shillings he was lost, and he much disliked half-crowns.

All these four types show disturbances of symbolic thinking and expression. In perfect symbolic thinking and expression it is necessary for words, numbers, pictures, and all they stand for in thought to be mobile and susceptible to perfect voluntary manipulation. Head's studies showed that in verbal and syntactical aphasia the idea of the structure of the words was what principally suffered in both external and internal speech. On the other hand in nominal and semantic defects the use of words in thinking and their manipulation and employment as language symbols was what was principally disturbed.

The more recent work of Weisenburg and McBride [1] has

[1] Weisenburg and McBride (13).

led to a somewhat different type of classification. One of the advantages of their work over Head's was that they made use of a control group of normal patients from the same economic and social classes as the aphasic patients, and of a similar educational and occupational level. The tests they used were far more extensive than those of Head, and since they had a control group it is possible to tell what performances are really typical of the aphasic patients and not merely actions which are occasionally performed by normal people as well.

They classified the aphasic disorders into four types like Head, but their types are somewhat different. They called them *expressive, receptive, expressive-receptive* and *amnesic*. The predominantly expressive group, which was the largest, showed defects in the articulation and formation of words, and in severe cases speech might be limited to a few utterances. Similar defects might extend to the patients' writing. These cases therefore are similar to Head's verbal-defect group. The predominantly receptive group showed a far more serious limitation in their understanding of spoken language or printed material. The patients frequently grasped a part of a statement and reacted on the basis of that : others might understand the specific words of the statement but fail to appreciate its whole significance. These, therefore, are like Head's semantic-defect group and also show some of the characteristics of his nominal-defect group. The expressive-receptive group were placed in a separate category because they showed a serious limitation of *all* their language performances. Sometimes the difficulty extended to non-language performances as well. The amnesic group which was the smallest is unlike the expressive group in that the people who suffered from the amnesic disorder were unable to evoke the necessary words as names for objects. They therefore, like the receptive group, show some of the characteristics of Head's nominal-defect group, though the receptive and the amnesic groups differ in the particular characteristics of the nominal-defect group with which they show a similarity.

Conclusion

An attempt has been made by Lévy-Bruhl [1] and others to show that the thought of the simpler peoples is qualitatively different from that of civilized peoples. Certainly when one takes the most emotional and irrational beliefs of the primitives and

[1] Lévy-Bruhl (6).

compares them with the highest forms of thought of civilized man there does appear to be a very noticeable qualitative difference. But enough has been said in this chapter to indicate that the thinking of civilized man—particularly in his superstitions and other emotionally-determined beliefs, in his occasional poverty of associations, slowness of associations and faulty organisation of associations—is often not far removed from that of primitive communities, and that the difference is perhaps best regarded as one of the degree or frequency with which emotional or rational beliefs are held.

REFERENCES

1. BENEDICT, R., *Patterns of Culture*. London : Routledge, 1935, pp. 291.
2. CURRAN, D., and GUTTMANN, E., *Psychological Medicine*. Edinburgh : Livingstone, 1943, pp. 188.
3. DEWEY, J., *How we Think*. New York : Heath, 1933, pp. 301.
4. FISHER, V. E., *An Introduction to Abnormal Psychology*. New York : Macmillan, 1931, pp. 512.
5. HEAD, H., *Aphasia and Kindred Disorders of Speech*. Cambridge : University Press, 1926, 2 vols.
6. LÉVY-BRUHL., L., *Primitive Mentality*. London : Allen & Unwin, 1923, pp. 458.
7. MAPOTHER, E., and LEWIS, A. J., " Psychological Medicine ". Sect. 21 of *A Textbook of the Practice of Medicine (Ed.*, F. W. Price). Oxford : University Press, 6th edn., 1941, pp. 2032.
8. MORGAN, J. J. B., *The Psychology of Abnormal People*. London : Longmans, Green, 1928, pp. 627.
9. STOUT, G. F., *Analytical Psychology*. London : Sonnenschein, 1902, 2 vols.
10. ——, *A Manual of Psychology*. London : University Tutorial Press, 4th edn., 1929, pp. 680.
11. THOULESS, R. H., *General and Social Psychology*. London : University Tutorial Press, 1937, pp. 522.
12. ——, *Straight and Crooked Thinking*. London : English Universities Press, 1938, pp. 284.
13. WEISENBURG, T., and McBRIDE, K. E., *Aphasia*. New York : Commonwealth Fund, 1935, pp. 634.
14. WOODWORTH, R. S., *Psychology*. London : Methuen, 12th edn., 1940, pp. 632.

CHAPTER IV

REMEMBERING

INTRODUCTORY

The older view about remembering was that it was essentially a reproductive process. This view was largely based on the somewhat arid experiments with nonsense syllables performed by Ebbinghaus [1] and his followers. One object of these experiments was to try to find some unit into which the higher mental processes could be analysed, and the theory of Ebbinghaus was that nonsense syllables would provide such a unit, for, unlike ordinary words, none of them had been associated in the mind with other words, and so they could be regarded as being equivalent. But the effect of this theory was that experiments were performed in highly artificial conditions, and although a number of deductions followed from them, notably in relation to the rapidity with which nonsense syllables were forgotten, there could be no possible justification for applying them to the processes of remembering as they exist in the situations of ordinary life. Remembering may be an essentially reproductive process so far as nonsense syllables are concerned, but what is really rather more important and interesting is to investigate what happens in remembering in less artificial conditions.

BARTLETT'S EXPERIMENTS

The series of experiments which has shown most clearly the mental processes involved in ordinary remembering is a series that has been done by Bartlett.[2] A large number of different experiments were performed with material of different kinds and with remembering of different kinds. In the first series (the *Method of Description*) the subjects were shown a series of five picture post-cards on each of which was the face of a sailor or soldier. As this experiment was done during the War of 1914-18 the series was of considerable interest to the people taking part in it. In the next series (the *Method of Repeated Reproduction*) the subjects were given a story or an argument in prose, or a simple drawing to study, and they had to reproduce it after an interval

[1] Ebbinghaus (7).   [2] Bartlett (4).

43

of fifteen minutes and subsequently at intervals of time of increasing length.   The object was to study the changes that might be introduced into reproductions with an increasing lapse of time. In the third series (the *Method of Picture Writing*) lists of more or less arbitrarily chosen signs had to be used by the subjects instead of the words with which the signs were given, the object being to find out from a series of repeated reproductions given over periods varying from one to nine months the changes or omissions in the signs that took place.   The fourth series was the *Method of Serial Reproduction*.   This method instead of studying the changes introduced into material by the same individual, studied the changes introduced into material by different individuals.   This is the kind of situation that exists when folk-tales are handed on from one person to another,[1] or when a rumour is passed from one individual to the next within the same social group.   The material was similar to that used in the *Method of Repeated Reproduction*.   It consisted of (*a*) folk-stories, (*b*) descriptive and argumentative material, and (*c*) picture material.   (*a*) and (*b*) were used as contrasts to each other, the former being material which belonged to a different social setting from that of the subjects doing the experiment, the latter being in a form which fitted into the subjects' own social setting, e.g. a description of a cricket match or a tennis game.

The experiments led to a number of general conclusions. Some of them had special reference to one or other of the different types of material, but no contradictions were found between them, and there was pronounced general agreement concerning the way in which the processes of remembering occurred.

In the first place the *order of sequence*, particularly in the *Method of Description*, was very liable to be disturbed.   The bearing that this has on the validity of evidence in a law court is important. It frequently happens that a particular point in a case turns on the question whether something happened before or after something else.   If it is generally found, as was found in the *Method of Description*, that one's memory for the order of events is specially undependable, it means that a person's evidence on such a point has to be treated very critically.

In the *Method of Reproduction*, however, the order of events was better preserved.   The material used in this method, it will be remembered, consisted of a series of temporally-related events arranged in the form of a narrative, whereas in the *Method of*

[1] See below, pp. 57-9.

Description the five objects had no logical temporal relationship. Even in the *Method of Repeated Reproduction*, however, there was evidence that an event of outstanding interest tended to be reproduced earlier in the recall than one which had no such outstanding character. As an example one can take the two excuses in the *War of the Ghosts* story. Two young men were being pressed to join a war party, and one of them used the following two excuses to avoid going. " One of the young men said, ' I have no arrows '. ' Arrows are in the canoe,' they said. ' I will not go along. I might be killed. My relatives do not know where I have gone. But you ', he said turning to the other, ' may go with them '." The story was being used at the time of the War of 1914–18 when a number of people were suffering from a conflict of motives about joining the fighting services or staying at home. Family ties was one of the strongest motives against joining up, and the fear of being killed was another. It was therefore natural that the second excuse should strike home more deeply than the first. The result was in general that either the first excuse was dropped altogether and only the second excuse remained in the reproductions, or else the order in which the excuses were given was reversed, the one bearing more emotional tone being the one which was given first.

Bartlett also noticed that there were a large number of *omissions*. In the *Method of Repeated Reproduction* and in the *Method of Serial Reproduction* the title of the story, proper names and definite numbers were commonly omitted. In the *Method of Picture Writing* signs not obviously or readily related to other material, or those not accorded a distinctive name, or even signs arousing a definite determination to remember were omitted. That is to say, the things that were most frequently omitted were those that the subjects found it difficult to organise with the rest of the material.[1]

Apart from omissions there were *inventions and importations*. In the *Method of Description* there was some tendency for the number of inventions to increase with lapse of time. This also occurred in the *Method of Repeated Reproduction* where it was noticed that the tendency to elaborate a story increased in the long-distance reproductions. In the picture material used in the *Method of Serial Reproduction* the inventions often took the form of a multiplication of detail in the designs. Sometimes, also, details were transferred from one point to another in the series ; this

frequently happened in connection with details which individual interest tended to make dominant.

Rationalisations [1] were sometimes applied to the story as a whole and sometimes to particular details within the story. They were particularly noticeable in the folk-stories belonging to a different social setting from that in which the individual lived. Rationalisation applied to particular details within a story sometimes took the form of connecting the events mentioned in the story with something supplied by the subject himself from outside, in order to make the point clear. At the end of the *War of the Ghosts* story, for example, after the young man had told his story, " When the sun rose he fell down. Something black came out of his mouth. His face became contorted. The people jumped up and cried. He was dead." The " something black " was often interpreted as a materialisation of the dying man's breath. On other occasions the process of rationalisation was more unwitting, as for instance when " something black " was transformed in one of the reproductions into " foamed at the mouth ", or when " canoe " was changed into " boat ", or " paddling " into " rowing ", or " peanut " into " acorn ". All these changes illustrate a process of changing something relatively unfamiliar into something more familiar, or of changing something not quite clear into something which is clearer, so as to get the material into a more explicable, straightforward and understandable form.

The same is true in the other type of rationalisation, rationalisation applied to the whole story. The folk-tales formed material which belonged to a different social setting and the subjects never accepted them immediately in their original form. Many of the events seemed to lack logical connection, and as they stood they appeared to be rather isolated from facts within the individual's experience. Therefore, the material was first of all labelled in some way, even though the labelling process might be no more than saying that a particular story was " not English ". But the process of labelling gave to the story its appropriate frame of reference, and in remembering it the subjects were subsequently guided by this frame of reference, and constructed their memory so as to fit in with it. Even after it had been labelled, however, the events in a story which lacked logical coherence were usually

---

[1] Since this term is used in the psychology of mental mechanisms in a rather different sense (see Chap. VIII), it might be better to employ another. The term suggested by Lindgren and Blackburn is *interpretation* (see p. 49).

also connected together so as to impose a coherence on the whole. The result was that after a few reproductions the story ceased to possess a jerky and inconsequential style, and was reduced to a logical and smoothly-related narrative.

Details which were outstanding tended to be remembered earlier than details which were not, as has already been mentioned. The reason a detail stood out depended partly on the affective tone it possessed. Other things that determined the outstanding character of a detail were (*a*) words or phrases that were currently popular : these would be particularly noticeable if they occurred in the course of a story which in the main possessed an unfamiliar setting and form, (*b*) anything comic or amusing, (*c*) material which fitted into the subjects' preformed interests and attitudes : in this case the details might be slightly transformed in the reproduction so as to make them fit even better, (*d*) some trivial things—although Bartlett found it was not possible to say which trivial things would be forgotten and which remembered, (*e*) things which were novel : these might be either unexpected details in an otherwise familiar form, or, as was seen above, a familiar detail in an otherwise unfamiliar setting.

All these points therefore show that in ordinary remembering the mental processes are very different from those involved in the remembering of nonsense syllables. Although in remembering lists of nonsense syllables a number of syllables are forgotten, yet importations and inventions have not been studied in the curve of forgetting ; rationalisations do not occur ; and the determination of outstanding detail is assumed to be dependent on the number of associations, if any, that may be attached to any particular syllable. Bartlett's experiments show the insufficiency of this hypothesis. They show that what really takes place in ordinary remembering is a *constructive* process, not merely a process of reproducing or dropping out associations. A person will remember a few outstanding details and construct the rest of his remembering around them. This was particularly noticeable in the *Methods of Repeated Reproduction* and of *Serial Reproduction*. A subject might remember the general style in which the story was written, label it " not English " and then try to reproduce the style by introducing into his recall unfamiliar words and phrases, which in fact took the reproduction further away from the original. Reproduction in the literal sense was a rare exception. Again, in the long-distance reproductions, e.g. after a period of some years, the subject would remember a few out-

standing details, some of which might be right and others wrong, and after he had recalled half a dozen or so of these he would use them as the basis for his story and construct the rest around them.

Sometimes the story underwent changes in successive reproductions. The changes were frequently towards a more familiar type of setting. Sometimes the changes were foreshadowed before they actually appeared, as, for instance, when a subject after finishing one of his reproductions remarked casually, " I have a sort of feeling that there was something about a rock, but I cannot fit it in." Although he did not fit it into this reproduction it occurred in the reproduction he gave two months later, there having been no rock in the original story.

In the case of reproductions with long intervals between them there were often constant changes towards simplification, omission, transformation, or elaboration, which went on almost indefinitely. However, when frequent reproductions were given with only a short interval between each, the constant changing of the story was much less noticeable. Here what usually happened was that once the first reproduction had been given, the general form of future reproductions was similar. In this case, therefore, the style of the reproduction rapidly became stereotyped.

Remembering in Non-artificial Situations

Bartlett's experiments, therefore, give us a clear idea of the processes of remembering. However, the subjects who took part knew—as is the case in nearly all psychological experiments—that they were in an experimental situation, and their results may have been affected accordingly, though to what extent and in what direction it is impossible to say. In remembering things in ordinary life we often do not know when we originally perceive an event that we will want to remember it later. In many cases, as for instance when we are suddenly called on to give evidence in a law court, we have to remember a thing that we did not particularly observe for the purpose of recalling it later. This is such a common situation that a series of experiments on remembering was done by Lindgren and Blackburn [1] under conditions in which the individuals were unaware at the time of the actual experiment that they were in an experimental situation. Without the knowledge of the people who were afterwards to be called upon to present an account Lindgren and Blackburn recorded the discussion following three meetings of the Cambridge

---

[1] As yet unpublished.

Psychological Society. After the third meeting they wrote to everyone who had been present at one or more of the meetings, and asked them to write down what they could remember about the discussions. A microphone was concealed in the room during one of the occasions and it was connected to a loudspeaker in an adjoining room where three shorthand writers took down the discussions. When the reports were received the results were analysed and it was found that after a period of a fortnight the average number of specific points remembered was only 8·4 per cent. of the total recorded. Furthermore, of this small amount on the average 42 per cent. were substantially incorrect. The incorrect material was of different kinds. In the first place there were *pure inventions*, statements about things that never took place in the discussion at all. Next there were *importations*, such as when an individual included in his report material that he might have obtained from his general reading but which did not occur in the course of the discussion. Next there were a large number of *muddles*, inspired by something that actually took place in the discussion, but which as presented in the subject's record was so confused and complicated and had so much false emphasis that the point recorded was far from being an accurate reproduction of the point that was made. *Inventions*, which also occurred, were sometimes attributable to a subject reacting emotionally to a point that occurred in the discussion. Then, in his recall, the bias caused by the emotional reaction led to the point being altered significantly. There were many *exaggerations*, and many instances of *elaboration* and *interpretation*, very similar to the kind of thing Bartlett found. One rather interesting type of invention was attributable to *inference*. A subject might invent a remark for a speaker which he knew the speaker habitually made, but which he did not happen to make on that particular occasion ; such, for example, as the formal thanking of the speaker by the chairman of the meeting. Sometimes the inference was in the form of making explicit in the recall a point that was only hinted at in the actual discussion, for example, by interpreting a remark which was intended to convey a particular impression, but which for reasons of tact, or for some other reason, the speaker did not express directly.

Another point of interest was that some of the subjects actually took part in the discussion while others did not. It was found that the average percentage of one's own remarks recalled to one's own remarks actually made was 23·0. On the other hand,

E

the average percentage of other people's remarks recalled to made was only 7·5. But although the number of one's own remarks recalled was greater than the number of other people's yet the recall of one's own remarks was sometimes more inaccurate than the recall of the same remark by another subject. The reason for this is probably that in remembering one's own remarks one is apt to interpret them. At the time at which they are made one knows what one wants to say, but from nervousness or inarticulateness, or for some other reason, one may not always express oneself as clearly and as accurately as one would like. In writing out the recall afterwards, however, when one has as much time as one wants at one's disposal, one can give a far more coherent, explicit and orderly account than when originally making the remark. This again shows the constructive character of remembering demonstrated in Bartlett's experiments. An individual is not so much concerned with the actual words he uses as with their general setting or frame of reference : it is the setting that he tends to reproduce in his recall, and he constructs his remembering about it.

A further experiment was performed with many of the same subjects. They were asked to describe a room with which they were familiar. The purpose was to compare memory for discussions with memory for objects. Similar things emerged. One noticeable feature was the prominence of inference. Things were put into the room which might quite easily have been there but which in fact were not. Furthermore, the inventions sometimes took the form of giving symmetrical descriptions. In the actual room, for example, there was a bookshelf on the west of the fireplace but none on the east, the fireplace being in the centre of the wall. Many of the subjects introduced a bookshelf on the east as well as the correct one on the west, and so gave a symmetrical appearance to that wall. Sometimes a particular feature of another room, such as a brick fireplace, was introduced into the description of the test room, and sometimes objects were invented without any discoverable reason.

In this experiment and in the discussion experiment one other point was interesting. There did not appear to be any agreement between subjective certainty and objective accuracy. An individual might be certain that a particular object was present in the room or that a particular event had occurred in the discussion when in fact no such object was present or no such event had occurred. Similarly, he might be very doubtful about the

presence of an object or the occurrence of an event when in fact it was present or had occurred.

All this is of interest from the point of view of the reliability of evidence in a court of law. Another application concerns the recording of psycho-analytic interviews. The point is brought out by Manson and Pear [1] who emphasise the fact that even if free associations are written down very faithfully they cannot always convey important characteristics such as are supplied by intonation and rhythm. Furthermore, if the Analyst merely writes down the free associations from memory afterwards what he writes down may suffer a double censorship, that of his own mind and that of the patient, and it is doubtful how far it can be relied upon to convey accurately what the subject originally said. The kind of alterations that may be made in the Analyst's recall (or in the patient's) are indicated in the experiments we have described above.

IMPAIRMENT OF MEMORY

The importance of the constructive processes in remembering can also be investigated in those individuals in whom the ability to organise material is impaired or obstructed in some way. One group of such cases occurs in patients who are suffering from some organic deterioration in their mental processes, such as general paralysis, senility or Korsakoff's syndrome.[2] In these the memory for recent events is usually far more impaired than is their memory for events which happened in their remote past, with the result that they are often disoriented in both time and space. They may maintain that they are at the moment not in a hospital in London but in the barracks at Gibraltar or in a ship in the Mediterranean or elsewhere where they may have spent some part of their earlier life. If they have such disorientation any events which take place tend to be interpreted in such a way as to fit in with this frame of reference. In this respect, therefore, they show some of the characteristics of the normal person who is constructing his recall round a frame of reference which happens to be incorrect, and they also show a certain similarity to the person suffering from a delusion, though as their false belief predominantly affects the memory processes it is convenient to treat it separately.

Sometimes, too, particularly in the Korsakoff case, the patients

[1] Manson and Pear (11).
[2] See, for example, Curran and Guttmann (6), p. 76 ; Mapother and Lewis (12), p. 1818.

try to cover up their defects in memory by a process known as *confabulation.* This may perhaps be regarded as an exaggeration of the tendency in normal remembering to fill in (often unwittingly) details which in fact have been forgotten, in order to present a complete and coherent picture of what it is that is being remembered. In the Korsakoff patient the most elaborate fabrications are often presented. But as these patients' memory for recent events is extremely weak, they may sometimes be found to have forgotten their most recent fabrication the moment after presenting it, with the result that they present a moment later another elaborate fabrication which is inconsistent with the first. Thus they appear to be highly suggestible. They are willing to accept a series of inconsistent suggestions made to them by other people, and to elaborate each one in turn. They act as if they were afraid of showing how poor their memory really is, so they take the first suggestion made to them and the next moment, having forgotten it, they may be elaborating a second suggestion inconsistent with the first. In this respect they show an exaggeration—a considerable exaggeration perhaps—of the process which many " normal " people exhibit when they are asked about something that they feel it is important for them to remember.

Another characteristic similar to the normal person which these patients show is that voluntary effort sometimes interferes with their ability to remember. It is a common experience of ordinary life that occasionally something one wants to remember seems to be more difficult to recall the more one tries to bring it into consciousness : but if one thinks about something else it may spontaneously and suddenly appear. So, too, the Korsakoff patient may remember more accurately and more fully when he is asked indirectly about a particular point than if the subject is approached directly. To this extent, therefore, there appears to be a certain amount of active inhibition or repression present, in addition to the physical deterioration.

FORGETTING

The fact that most remembering takes place on a constructive basis by organising an event round what is considered to be its frame of reference leads to the question of forgetting and to the question what things are most likely to be forgotten. Freud [1] has put forward the view that repression plays an important part in the forgetting of ordinary life. In his view it is linked with things

[1] Freud (8).

that we want to forget but which we do not like consciously to admit that we want to forget, " Forgetting in all cases is proved to be founded on a motive of displeasure." [1] Furthermore, if a particular fact is not available to consciousness at a given moment the reason is that it has been repressed into the unconscious. Freud gives a number of illustrations of the kind of thing he means, thus if we have an unpleasant letter to answer we tend to put off answering it as long as we can, and then when finally we bring ourselves to answer it we may find we have mislaid it and thus have no record of the address to which our answer should be sent. Misprints, malapropisms and spoonerisms are often attributable to the same mechanism in Freud's view, for instance, a news-paper referring to a particular general of whom it disapproved called him " that bottle-scarred veteran ", only to apologise next day by saying that what they really meant to say, of course, was, " that battle-scared veteran ". Freud's view is that if an individual who has apparently forgotten something is psycho-analysed it will become available again, and this shows that he has never really forgotten it. Certainly it is true that by the use of psycho-analysis or by the use of hypnotism many more things can be made available than are available to the conscious mind, but this of course does not prove that nothing is ever forgotten. Freud's view is perhaps not so universally applicable as is claimed by the Freudians, but at the moment it is as impossible to refute as it is to prove.

In view of the experimental work which has already been discussed, however, it would seem to be likely that one reason why we forget things is that they will not fit into the frame of reference we have constructed for ourselves, and that they appear to have no relationship to it : or that their form has to be so altered in order to make them fit into the frame of reference that their individuality becomes lost. That is to say, events may undergo so much transformation in order to make them fit in with other events that their original form is " forgotten ". Cases of this kind were noticed both in Bartlett's and in Lindgren and Blackburn's experiments, and they are confirmed by the experience of ordinary life. After seeing a reconstructed building or street it is often difficult to remember what it looked like before the reconstruction had taken place. [2]

[1] Freud, (8) p. 138.
[2] For a fuller discussion of this and other related points, see Koffka (9), Chaps. 10 and 11.

Another reason for forgetting is when an event possesses no individuality of its own, nothing that leads it to be organised as an event separate from, though related to, others. For example, if one has the habit of winding up one's watch every night before retiring to bed, one will sometimes find on getting into bed that one is not sure whether one has wound it up that night or not. The fact that the particular action has been done so often and in the same way means that any one instance has no individuality of its own, nothing that enables it to stand out from the other similar actions.

This may be one explanation also why lists of nonsense syllables are more difficult to learn than lists of ordinary words. Nonsense syllables are so much more like one another, they mean so much less than ordinary words that we find difficulty in organising them so as to be able to remember them. The point was brought out in some experiments performed by Von Restorff [1] in which nonsense syllables were readily remembered when they were presented in lists composed of one nonsense syllable and nine numbers, but they were very frequently forgotten when they were presented in lists composed entirely of heterogeneous material, e.g. a number, a nonsense syllable, a colour, a letter, a word, a photograph, a symbol, a button, a punctuation mark, and a name of a chemical compound. That is to say, the nonsense syllables were best remembered when they occurred as isolated elements in a list and could be organised as isolated elements different from the other members of the list. When they did not occur as isolated elements, when they could not be organised separately, they tended to be forgotten.

All the same, emotional factors undoubtedly play a part in creating some types of forgetting, and repression probably plays a rather bigger part than many people are willing to admit. In a somewhat extreme form forgetting what we unconsciously want to forget is seen in certain hysterical disorders, e.g. fugues or " loss of memory " cases. In these the patients may forget who they are and what they have been doing, and they sometimes wander off to another locality. In some cases they adopt an entirely new kind of life for a while, though they may appear to be normal to their acquaintances in their new environment. Sometimes in these cases the patients will " come to them-selves " after a while and be very surprised to find themselves in a strange environment, wearing strange clothes and engaged in an

[1] Von Restorff (15).

unfamiliar type of work. So far as they can recollect, the last thing that happened to them occurred just before the onset of the fugue, and they have no conscious memory for any of the events which have occurred in the intervening period. In other cases the patients are found wandering by the police, and they are unable to give an adequate account of themselves. When such cases are examined there is usually found to be a sufficient reason to account for the onset of the disorder—some situation from which the patient wishes to escape, although he is unable to admit this fact into his conscious mind. Such amnesic phenomena usually lie close to the surface of consciousness and they are thus relatively easy to bring into the patient's conscious mind by some technique such as hypnotism. In the same way, too, it is possible to *produce* amnesias by the use of hypnotism. In these cases the patient may be persuaded to behave as if he were somebody else, or to have a complete or a partial amnesia for what has taken place while he was hypnotised. In all these cases, therefore, we see a process of active repression at work, so that the resulting memory either contains unfilled gaps, or else the gaps are filled by false inferences and fabrications.

Déjà vu

A slightly more complex situation arises with the phenomenon of *déjà vu*. This is the feeling which many normal individuals sometimes experience of having " been there before ". They go to some place, or they hold a conversation, and while they are there or while they are conversing they feel convinced that they have been in that place or held that conversation at some time in the past, although they cannot recall exactly when it was. A number of explanations have been offered to account for the phenomenon. The most probable explanation seems to be that what is actually happening is that the present situation bears some similarity with a situation that occurred in the past, but that it has some differences as well. The individual experiencing the feeling of familiarity notices the similarities but represses the differences, and this active repression gives him the feeling of strangeness about the situation. Some light on the question was thrown by an interesting experiment performed by Banister and Zangwill.[1] Three similar sets of picture post-cards were prepared

---

[1] Banister and Zangwill (1). Note that these authors are doubtful of the validity of applying the results of their experiments to a general theory of *déjà vu*.

and on the first day the people on whom the experiment was performed were shown the first series and asked to describe it. On the second day they were deeply hypnotised, shown the second series, asked to describe it and then told that they would not recognise it if it were shown to them again. On the third day they were shown a set of cards some of which they had seen two days previously under normal conditions, some of which they had seen the day before under deep hypnosis, and some of which were new to them. The three sets of cards were presented by different examiners, and the examiner on the third day had no knowledge which of the cards had been presented on either of the preceding days nor which were new. The subjects' reactions were characteristic. Those they had seen two days before under ordinary conditions they at once remembered having seen and said so : those that were new they described in the kind of way they had described the first set on the first day of the experiment. But with those they had been shown when hypnotised and told they would not remember again their behaviour was completely different. They hesitated and fidgeted and sometimes sweated : they started sentences and then stopped abruptly. " This card makes a great impression on me. I wonder who the lady is ? Ghosts. It reminds me of a phrase people sometimes say : ' I am sure you said that before ', or ' I am sure I have heard it before ', or ' I knew you were going to say that '." Another example was, " I have the impression . . . I have the impression that I have seen that before . . ." (*pause*). The examiner then said, " *Do you remember where or anything about it ?* " The answer was, " I have a feeling I should like to tell you, but why can't I say it ? I have the same feeling as I had . . . I know exactly. . . . There is something in my mind which is making continual efforts to tell you but my tongue won't get on with the job. Now where did I ? I am just saying to myself now : ' Come on, don't be so dumb ! You know you have seen it before ' . . . It's like making up one's mind to jump over one of those walls that give way under you—those dry walls in Yorkshire—I simply can't give you the answer. It's a very tiring process too." Thus here one sees a very similar picture to that presented by a person who is experiencing the feeling of familiarity in *déjà vu*, and here the conditions under which the experiment was performed were very carefully controlled and known to the experimenter.

REMEMBERING AND THE FOLK-TALE

Apart from the light they throw on remembering as a constructive process Bartlett's experiments also indicate the importance of *social* processes in the matter and in the manner of recall.
They throw an important light in particular on the psychological
processes at work behind the origin and development of folk-
tales, myths, legends, traditional stories and so on. In another
place Bartlett [1] has mentioned some of the tendencies which
influence the form of the popular tale and which subsequently
influence the transformations which the story undergoes in the
course of repetition. It is particularly determined by those
impulses which come into operation when a man becomes the
centre of attention of a group of his fellows. One of these is
the tendency to secure dramatic effects or to create astonishment
and wonder. Many examples of this can be given.[2] Thus the
hero is often the youngest son or an orphan or a widow's son,
while the heroine is ill-treated by a stepmother or stepsisters.
This enhances the melodramatic effect of the *dénouement* at the
end. Or, again, the hero, with an enviable combination of
intrepidity and astuteness, disenchants a haunted castle ; or cuts
off the giant hand which reaches down the chimney to carry off
every new-born babe ; or discovers the formula for reawakening
the bewitched princess ; or performs some other action of this
kind involving the thrill of adventure.

A second tendency is to produce laughter. This tendency is
less obvious than the first, and the form of the tale is more often
striking for its melodramatic than for its humorous situations.
Nevertheless it often makes its appearance. The hero is often
a dunce (and a widow's son into the bargain) who achieves a
successful career more by good fortune than by acts of bravery ;
or sometimes he is a person with rather low moral and ethical
standards, without strength and without courage, who achieves
his end by shrewdness and cunning.

Both of these types of tale—the melodramatic and the
humorous—are likely to be subjected in the course of transmission
to many of the processes which were disclosed in Bartlett's experiments. In addition the elements of both types of story are likely
to be exaggerated as they are passed on in order to enhance their
effect. Now although both types of story may be found, the
question whether one rather than the other type predominates

---

[1] Bartlett (2).   [2] See, for example, Krappe (10), Chap. 1.

will depend very largely on the customs and beliefs, the interests, tendencies, attitudes and sentiments prevalent in different communities—according, that is to say, to their cultural pattern. Bartlett himself gives an example of this.[1] The Zulu, in recalling material which concerns methods of conducting warfare is excited and voluble and full of interest ; the Swazi on the same topic is quiet and reticent and bored. But in recalling material concerning diplomatic cunning—which plays or played a large part in the Swazi pattern of culture—it is the Swazi who is confident and voluble and interested, the Zulu who is quiet and bored. Other examples may be given.

Before we turn to this, however, let us consider one more characteristic feature of many folk-tales. This is what Bartlett [2] has called " primitive comradeship ". The community is held together by its reaction against constraint : sympathy and friendship and social solidarity are praised as the greatest of virtues. The normal difference between men and animals disappears. They intermarry. The one helps the other. There is a bond between them. But again the prevalence of this type of tale will be conditioned by the cultural pattern of different communities. In those where primitive comradeship is strong this type of tale is likely to be more frequent than in those where it is weak.

Geographical factors also play a part, but in their case the effect is more inhibitory than creative. Let us take as an example of this a well-known folk-tale. The bear in Northern Europe is one of the few tailless animals. The question that quite naturally arises is " Why ? ", and the answer that springs to the mind is, " Because he lost it ". Then how did he come to lose it ?—and in answer to this we get the story of the fox who persuaded the bear to dip his tail into the water one winter night in order to catch fish, how the water froze, and how the bear in pulling himself free left his tail behind. But when this story is repeated in areas where there are no bears it becomes somewhat pointless. Since, however, the story as such may be interpreted differently as a good example of cunning (represented by the fox), it is that aspect which tends to remain and to be transmitted in social remembering. Thus for the bear the wolf comes to be substituted, an animal known in areas where the bear is unknown, and although the wolf does have a tail, yet the characteristic feature of the cunning of the fox is unaffected by this minor detail.

Again the influence of the cultural pattern may be seen in the

[1] Bartlett (4), pp. 263-4.   [2] Idem (3), pp. 37 et seq.

type of task which the hero has to perform in order to win his bride. Sometimes he has to win a race, sometimes a duel, sometimes a pugilistic match, sometimes a game of chess, or sometimes he has to solve some riddles. The task which is preferred is likely to be determined by the predominant tendencies of different communities. Thus in Iceland or Ireland a boxing match is often the preferred type of test ; in India and the East it is more often a game of chess.

Much remains to be done in disentangling the influence of the cultural pattern on the form of the folk-tale. At the present time perhaps the most fruitful investigation has been made by Boggs.[1] Among Boggs' interesting results may be cited the following. *Animal stories* are twice as popular among the Lapps as they are among the Finns. *Religious tales* dealing with Christ, the Virgin, Saints, etc., are least frequent in Finland, 97 per cent. of whose inhabitants are Protestant, while they are most frequent in Spain, the most Catholic of countries. In Hungary more than half of all tales are *magic tales*, i.e. tales about some supernatural or enchanted person or thing : the next highest country, Norway, is considerably lower, while Spain ranks very low indeed. *The girl as helper in the hero's flight* is very popular in Norway, Rumania, Hungary, and Spain : it is rare in Finland and unknown in Flanders. Tales about a *supernatural or enchanted husband, wife or other relative* are very frequent in Norway and least frequent in Spain. (Incidentally enchanted wives are more popular than enchanted husbands.) *Stupid ogre* tales abound in Finland and Lapland and they are common in Norway, but they are infrequent elsewhere. *Jokes and anecdotes* are most popular in Flanders, but they are relatively infrequent in Norway, Rumania and Spain, and very infrequent in Lapland and Hungary. Everywhere, however, jokes and anecdotes about men far outnumber those about women.

This, then, is as far as present research will take us. Much remains to be done—work that is of vital interest to the social psychologist—before a more comprehensive picture of the influence of the cultural pattern on the matter and the manner of social recall will finally emerge.

[1] Boggs (5).

REFERENCES

1. BANISTER, H., and ZANGWILL, O. L., " Experimentally induced Visual Paramnesias ". *Brit. J. Psychol.*, 1941, **32**, 30–51.
2. BARTLETT, F. C., "Psychology in Relation to the Popular Story ". *Folklore*, 1920, **30**, 264–93.
3. ——, *Psychology and Primitive Culture.* Cambridge : University Press, 1923, pp. 294.
4. ——, *Remembering.* Cambridge : University Press, 1932, pp. 317.
5. BOGGS, R. S., " A Comparative Survey of the Folk-tales of 10 Peoples ". *FF Communications*, 1930, **33**, No. 93, pp. 14.
6. CURRAN, D., and GUTTMANN, E., *Psychological Medicine.* Edinburgh : Livingstone, 1943, pp. 188.
7. EBBINGHAUS, H., *Memory.* New York : Teachers' College, Columbia University, 1913, pp. 123.
8. FREUD, S., *The Psychopathology of Everyday Life.* London : Unwin, 6th edn., 1920, pp. 342.
9. KOFFKA, K., *Principles of Gestalt Psychology.* London : Kegan Paul, 1935, pp. 720.
10. KRAPPE, A. H., *The Science of Folk-Lore.* London : Methuen, 1920, pp. 344.
11. MANSON, R. H., and PEAR, T. H., " The Testimony of Conversation ". *Brit. J. Psychol.*, 1937, **27**, 277–91.
12. MAPOTHER, E., and LEWIS, A. J., " Psychological Medicine ". Sect. 21 of *A Textbook of the Practice of Medicine (Ed.,* F. W. Price). Oxford : University Press, 6th edn., 1941, pp. 2032.
13. MORGAN, J. J. B., *The Psychology of Abnormal People.* London : Longmans, Green, 1928, pp. 627.
14. PEAR, T. H., *Remembering and Forgetting.* London : Methuen, 1922, pp. 242.
15. RESTORFF, H. VON., " Uber die Wirkung von Beruchsbildung im Spurenfeld ". *Psychol. Forsch.*, 1933, **18**, 299–342.

CHAPTER V

INTELLIGENCE AND ABILITY

INTRODUCTORY

Intelligence, like electricity, is easier to talk about than to define. When we think of the word we all have some vague idea about what we mean by it, though different people may mean different things, and so may the same person at different times. When one comes to try to define it many difficulties arise. It may be agreed, perhaps, that dull people are usually backward, but the converse of this proposition is often far from being true : all backward people are not dull, for the experiences and training to which they have been subjected may have been such as to deny fruition to their best qualities. Then, too, the ordinary man uses the word *intelligence* differently at different times : sometimes he uses it in the sense of an infinite capacity to take pains : sometimes to the playing on the emotions of one person by another in order to get what he wants : sometimes to witty conversation : sometimes to an almost shady transaction, and so on. Even psychologists themselves working in different fields have used it differently : the teacher tends to regard it as a power to acquire learning : the psychiatrist as a power to think abstractly : the animal psychologist as the ability to adapt behaviour to ever-changing conditions, and so on. Owing to the multiplicity of uses the psychologist who attempts to measure intelligence is obliged to define it in his own way. But here again different approaches have been made, and tests based on different principles have been devised.

THE TESTING OF INTELLIGENCE

At the beginning of the century Alfred Binet was invited by the educational authorities in Paris to devise a series of tests through which the children who would not be able to profit by the training given in the ordinary elementary schools in Paris could be eliminated. As a result of this request Binet published in 1905 [1] a scale of questions based on some of the different kinds of practical situations that children might be expected to encounter in the course of their ordinary everyday lives. It was a practical

---

[1] Binet and Simon (2).

problem he was faced with, and he thought it could best be solved by, as it were, taking a series of borings at different points. That is to say by basing his tests on a series of diverse situations and then discovering the average level of performance in these different tests. Assuming that the children had all had more or less the same background of experiences, then, although some might be more familiar than others with some of his situations, yet they might be expected to be less familiar with others, and on the average these different experiences might be expected to cancel out, so that the average score would indicate with a fair degree of accuracy their general level of ability. The better they could adapt themselves to and solve these problems the higher would be their score.

Binet obtained his scale by devising a series of representative questions, and then putting them to a large number of children of different ages. In this way the questions could be arranged in " mental ages " corresponding to the ages of the children who could pass them. And Binet arranged that in the scale which emerged there were several tests for each mental age. Then, having devised the scale, he was able to apply it to other children and their results could be compared with the results derived from the children of the same chronological age on whom the tests had been standardised.

Here are a few examples from Burt's revision of Binet's test.[1] A child aged 4 should be able to repeat correctly three digits which are read out to him. A child of 6 should be able to define correctly in terms of use at least four of the following six things :— chair, horse, fork, doll, picture, table. A child aged 8 should be able to count backwards correctly from 20 to 1. A child aged 11 should be able to say correctly what is absurd about three out of five statements similar to the following : " A soldier writing a letter to his mother started like this, ' Dear Mother, I am writing this with a sword in one hand and a pistol in the other '." And a child aged 15 should be able to repeat backwards six digits read out to him.

Out of Binet's work arose his important concept of mental age (M.A.). The child of 9 should theoretically be able. to pass all the tests up to and including the ones designed for age IX (M.A.) [2] but should fail in every test for a later age. In practice this is rarely found to be the case, for the child some-

---

[1] Burt (3).
[2] Mental age is usually shown by Roman numerals, chronological age by Arabic.

times fails on a few tests below those for his age and succeeds on a few above. In order to estimate his mental age, therefore, one credits him with the mental age corresponding to the highest year for which he passes all the tests, adds the appropriate fraction of a year for the proportion of tests passed in higher ages and subtracts the appropriate fraction for tests failed at lower years. Thus, if a child passes all the tests for age VIII, three out of six for age IX, one out of six for age X and none for higher ages, he will have a mental age of VIII years + VI months + II months = VIII years VIII months. If, in spite of passing all the tests for age VIII the same child failed in one out of the six tests for age VII but in none of the tests for lower ages which he may have been given, his mental age will be VIII years VI months.

In order to make the comparison between children of different mental ages easy Stern and Terman subsequently proposed the adoption of the term " Intelligence Quotient " (I.Q.). This is obtained from the fraction

$$\frac{\text{M.A.}}{\text{C.A.}} \times 100 \text{ (where C.A.} = \text{Chronological Age)}.$$

A child of 8 with a mental age of X will therefore have an I.Q. of 125 which is the same as that of a child of 10 with a mental age of XII years VI months. And a child of 10 with a mental age of VIII years VI months will have the same I.Q (85) as a child of 13 with a mental age of XI. Fractions are ignored, the I.Q. being given to the nearest integer.

Spearman's [1] approach to the testing of intelligence was different from Binet's. He did not start with a practical problem but he began with an analysis of what he was going to mean by intelligence. For him it appeared to be the ability to grasp complex relationships between objects, and he and his followers have devised tests on this assumption. As a result of his researches he declared as early as 1904 that " all branches of intellectual activity have in common one fundamental function (or group of functions) whereas the remaining or specific elements seem in every case to be different from that in all the others ". He named this common function " g " and proposed to abandon the term " intelligence " because it had " so many meanings that finally it has none ". Whereas g is common to all intellectual processes s is specific to each process.

[1] Spearman (15).

Examples of the kind of test used to measure *g* are the following. The examples are very simple, but they can be made of any degree of complexity or difficulty.

Analogies .	. *Black* is to *white* as *big* is to—
	HEAVY, BRIGHT, LITTLE, MAN
Synonyms and	*Ill* means the same or nearly the same as
Antonyms .	. BEAUTIFUL, FINE, BRIGHT, UNWELL
	Good is the opposite of—
	WHITE, BAD, TINY, FALSE
Mixed Sentences .	Through air birds the fly—TRUE, FALSE
Classification .	The person being tested is required to underline the word which is in a different category from the others—
	CHAIR, TABLE, WHEAT, RUG, CURTAIN
Number Series .	The person being tested is required to pick out the two numbers which continue the following series—
	1, 3, 5, 7, 9, . . . 10, 11, 12, 13, 14
Codes .	. A message has to be transcribed according to some principle, such as that each letter must be represented by the letter that precedes it in the alphabet.
Inferences .	. *Jack* is taller than *Bill* but not so tall as *Tommy*. Which is the tallest ?—
	JACK, BILL, TOMMY

Spearman's theory is based on mathematical and statistical analysis whereas Binet's is based on the solving of a particular kind of practical problem. The two types of test are therefore selected on rather different principles. Those which are best for Spearman's theory are those which fulfil his mathematical criteria most accurately ; those which are best for Binet are those which are most accurate in eliminating ineducable children from the elementary school. With this difference the two types of test might be measuring entirely different things. In fact, however, they are not, for there is usually a fair correlation between their results.

A third approach to the testing of intelligence has been suggested by Kent.[1] Kent's view is that the most accurate results cannot be obtained if a single composite scale is given to every child being tested, for the scale will inevitably be unfair to some children compared with others. Kent therefore suggests that a number of different units should be developed, each unit consisting of items which can be graded in difficulty, arranged in

[1] Kent (8).

a series, and standardised independently of the other units. Then the person giving the test would be in the position of being able to select only those units which were best suited to the person being tested, and the test situation would be arranged so as to fit the person being tested instead of, as at present, the person being tested being expected to fit the test. Her view is that intelligence cannot be measured as an entity, but only as a type of behaviour. No physician would rely on a diagnosis of his patient in terms of a " physical quotient ", and similarly no psychologist ought to be content to express his report in terms of an intelligence quotient, for mental characteristics are quite as variable as physical. The psychologist should, therefore, according to this view, base his comparison between individuals on differences in their behaviour judged by the kind of test in which they do well or badly, rather than on their possession of a few points more or less of whatever it may be that is measured by an intelligence test scale.

A further disadvantage of the tests which have been discussed up to now is that they almost all depend on words and the use of language. This fact may affect the scores of people with a greater or smaller degree of fluency in the use of the language in which the test is given.[1] It is still more obvious in the case of people who are completely illiterate.

In an attempt to overcome this difficulty various attempts have been made to produce tests of a non-verbal type. One example is Sleight's non-verbal intelligence test designed for children between the ages of 6 and 10 years. The ten component tests include substitution, classification, series continuation and other types arranged in the form of pictures and drawings. For instance, instead of the words " TRUMPET, TABLE, VIOLIN, DRUM ", pictures of these objects are presented, and the child is told to mark a ring round the object that is in a different class from the others. The test is thus based on the same principles as have already been discussed, but the form in which it is given differs.

Leiter [2] has devised a scale which is intended to be as far as possible independent of cultural background. It consists of two tests for each year between the ages of V and X and one for each year from XI to XVI. Its principle is the matching of appropriate designs. In a test for year VII, for example, a strip on

---

[1] For a fuller discussion of this point see my forthcoming book, *The Framework of Human Behaviour*.
[2] Leiter (10).

which five graduated circles are drawn is placed before the person being tested, and he is given also five bricks on each of which is drawn a square of different size.   He has to arrange the squares in a graduated series corresponding to that of the circles drawn on the strip.   This test, together with a line completion test, is illustrated in Fig. 15.

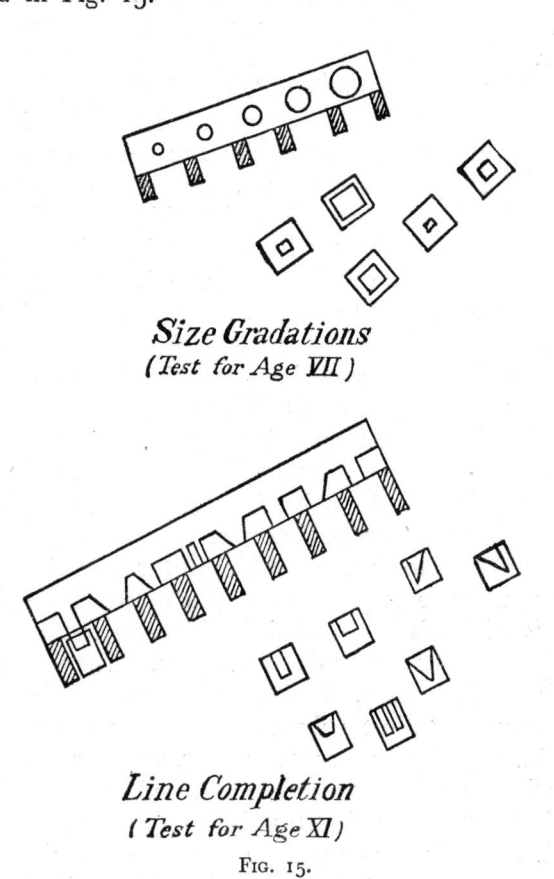

Size Gradations
(*Test for Age* VII)

Line Completion
(*Test for Age* XI)

Fig. 15.

Different principles are involved in the " matrices " test developed by Penrose and Raven.[1] This test has become of increasing importance since its widespread use in the testing of personnel of the Navy and Army during the present war.   The series is based on the analogies type of verbal test, and the general structure may contain four or nine elements, or be even

[1] Penrose and Raven (13).

more complex. The structure containing four elements is of the general form :

$$A \qquad f(A)$$
$$f'(A) \qquad f'f(A)$$

If the eyes move horizontally the right-hand figure is seen to bear a certain relationship to the left-hand figure, whereas if they move vertically the lower figure is seen to bear a similar type

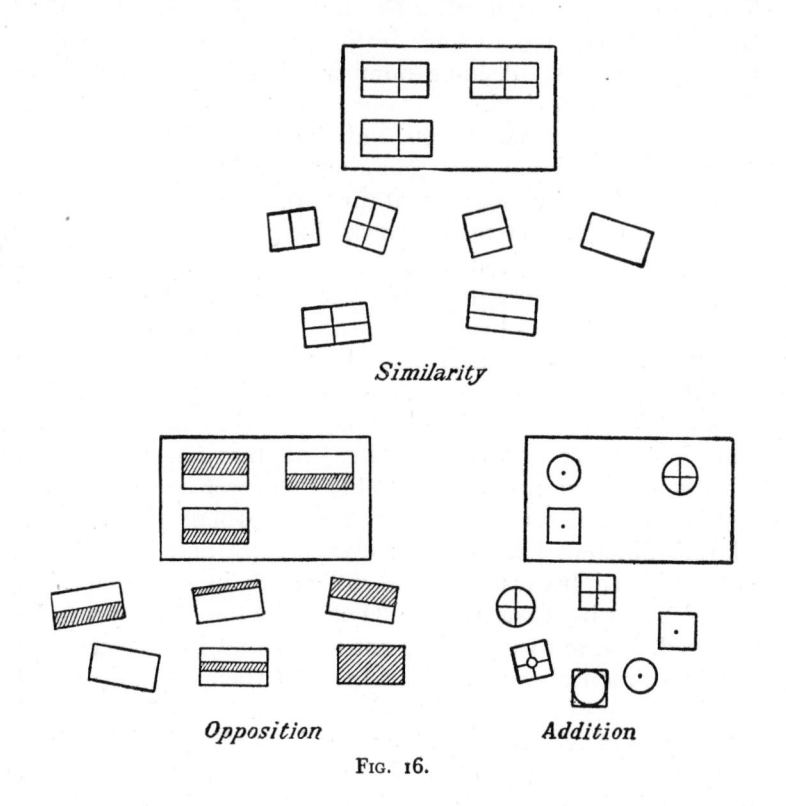

Similarity

Opposition   *Addition*

FIG. 16.

of relationship to the upper figure. The relationship may be one of similarity, opposition or addition (see Fig. 16). The person being tested is presented with a booklet containing the graded series of tests. In the simplest form there may be three figures and a blank space. Underneath the figures are a number of different designs. The person being tested has to select the figure bearing the correct design, so that the analogy between the designs is completed. The required answer can be inferred by making either horizontal or vertical comparisons. More complicated

relationships are involved when the structure contains nine elements. The person being tested must notice that whatever occurs in both the first and second rows or columns determines what occurs in the third, and thus arrive at the ninth figure.

A number of other tests of a non-verbal nature are commonly referred to as " performance tests of intelligence ". They were originally devised to test deaf children, illiterates and foreigners. Here the person being tested is usually presented with some kind of puzzle that he has to solve by putting the pieces into their appropriate places. A large number of different performance tests have been devised.[1]

Although performance tests and the matrices test have the advantage over verbal tests that they dispose of the language factor, it has yet to be shown that they are unaffected by cultural influences. It has yet to be shown that individuals given one type of education rather than another, or individuals who belong to different racial groups within the same community or in different communities [2] suffer from no disadvantage or gain no advantage over other individuals in tests of this type. It is sometimes too readily assumed—particularly in regard to matrices or to performance tests—that intelligence tests are measuring innate intelligence and nothing else. All that has been shown in fact is that they measure the ability to answer intelligence test questions, and any comparison between groups of people who have had very different backgrounds of experience may be more or less invalidated because of these differences in experience. A test which has been *proved* to be " culturally free " has yet to be developed. Nevertheless this is not to say that intelligence tests are of no practical value. Provided that their limitations and possible sources of error are properly understood and remembered they may be of very considerable value in grading individuals or groups who are known to have had very much the same general background of education and training. It should not, however, be uncritically assumed that if a psychologist defines intelligence as something innate (which he has every justification for doing if he thinks it helps) his intelligence tests must of necessity accurately measure the amount of innate intelligence which a person possesses. What he measures may be something rather different from what he has defined.

[1] See, for example, Pintner and Paterson (14), Arthur (1), Drever and Collins (5).
[2] For a discussion of the whole question of racial differences and of the effect of the environment on intelligence test scores, see my forthcoming book, *The Framework of Human Behaviour*.

THE GROWTH AND DECLINE OF TEST INTELLIGENCE

The limitations of intelligence tests need to be particularly borne in mind when one is testing the intelligence of adults. So far as children are concerned it is relatively easy to determine whether or not they differ significantly in the background of education and training to which they have been subjected. But most adults, after they have left school, abandon the kind of competitive tasks which form the basis of school work to take up other kinds of competitive tasks which form the basis of working life in our community. Are intelligence tests which often bear a close similarity to the competitive tasks of school likely, therefore, to give a fair picture, or a comparable picture, when they are given to adults?

The point arises when one considers the growth and decline of test intelligence. When a child is re-tested on an intelligence test after a lapse of time there is usually a fairly close agreement between his I.Q. on the two occasions. His actual score on the test is higher on the second occasion, but his mental ratio represented by the I.Q. remains about the same. This indicates that the *amount* of intelligence he possesses, like his height, increases as he gets older, rapidly at first but more and more gradually as he approaches puberty, although his *level* of test intelligence remains the same. It has frequently been shown that the test intelligence of the normal child stops increasing at about the age of 15 years. The test intelligence of subnormal children stops increasing earlier than this—at about the age of 12 years— while that of superior children continues until the age of about 18 years or later.

Two methods have been used to get a picture of mental growth. One is to re-test a group of children several times as they grow older. This is a laborious method as well as being very time-consuming. It also has the disadvantage that a practice effect of unknown dimensions may enter into the scores on the second and subsequent occasions, with the result that these scores may become unreliable. For even though the children are not given exactly the same tests on the different occasions, they acquire a greater familiarity with intelligence test situations in general, and may develop an improved technique of dealing with them—they acquire, that is to say, a " test sophistication " which helps to raise their scores above what they would otherwise be. (Incidentally psychologists possess this test

sophistication in a very marked degree. It may be that without it their scores on intelligence tests would be much lower, and that in consequence they would not regard them with quite the same degree of veneration.)

The more usual method is to test a large number of people of different ages at the same time, and to regard the average scores of each age group as indicating the normal course of development at the different ages. This has the disadvantage that precautions have to be taken to ensure that all the age groups are of similar composition and that they are all truly representative of the population being tested. In particular, the older age groups may suffer from more physical handicaps, e.g. defective eyesight, difficulties in reading and so on, which will handicap their test performance. It also has the disadvantage— if the age span being tested is a wide one—that the methods of teaching and of schooling may have undergone a considerable change from one generation to the next, so there will be nothing to guarantee that the levels presented by the upper age groups now will be the same as those which the younger generation will indicate in thirty or forty or fifty years' time.

Both methods suffer from the disadvantage that precisely the same abilities may not be being tested at the different ages. Tests which are appropriate for younger children have to differ quite considerably in content from those appropriate at the upper age levels. All that the existing mental growth curves can be relied upon to indicate, therefore, is either (when the first method is used) the general course of development that may be expected under certain cultural conditions, or (when the second method is used) a picture of the levels of individuals of different ages within a particular group—and not a very reliable one at that. With these limitations in mind, let us turn to the picture presented by mental growth curves. One of the best known is that of Miles and Miles.[1] They tested 823 people whose ages ranged from 7 to 94 years. Table I shows the average of 617 adults in this experiment.

The averages show practically no change between the ages of 15 and 34. Between 35 and 54 there is a slow but consistent decline. After 55 the decline is more rapid, and it continues up to the oldest age group tested.[2]

---

[1] Miles and Miles (11).
[2] In the later age groups physiological factors connected with senility undoubtedly play a part in causing the decline in test intelligence.

TABLE I.—RELATION BETWEEN TEST SCORE AND CHRONOLOGICAL AGE

Age.	Number.	Average.
15–24	91	38·2
25–34	83	37·2
35–44	92	34·5
45–54	105	31·9
55–64	106	28·4
65–74	95	23·9
75–84	39	18·5
85–94	6	15·3

Other investigations have shown similar results, but before we conclude—even within the limitations we have imposed on ourselves—that they represent a truly comparable picture of the levels of individuals of different ages within a particular group, there are a few final points that need to be made. In the first place the standard deviation [1] of the scores in the higher age levels is considerably greater than that in the lower. This may be a reflection of the effect of the greater range of experiences to which adults are subject—increasing the heterogeneity of the adult group the older they become.

Then again Willoughby,[2] investigating family similarities in mental characteristics, showed that after adulthood the different tests he used presented very different pictures. Tests like series completion, opposites, codes, and analogies showed a marked decline with age, whereas reasoning involving arithmetic showed no decline. The cause is presumably that arithmetical reasoning is a useful task which continues to be employed in everyday life after school has been left. Similarly, too, the decline of the scores of the older age groups in the other tests might be attributable to the degree of remoteness of the members of the older age groups from formal schooling, since the subject matter of these tests does not enter into the ordinary life of adults to nearly the same extent as it does into school life, except in relatively infrequent cases.

Finally, in Miles and Miles' investigation when curves for decline were plotted for four different groups, namely—

A. Those who had had four years of college, together with additional graduate or professional training ;

B. Those who had had one year or more at college (including those in group A) ;

---

[1] The standard deviation is a statistical measurement of the scatter of scores about their average. A high standard deviation indicates a wide range of scores ; a low standard deviation indicates that the scores are close together.

[2] Willoughby (19).

C. Those who had had only one to four years of high school or its equivalent ;

D. Those who had had only eight or fewer grades of elementary school ;

it was found that although all the groups showed a decline with age, yet the decline was much smaller for those who had had more education than for those who had had less. In fact the lowest point reached by group A was higher than the highest points reached by groups C and D. Thus a person who was 70 years old and who had undertaken at least one year of post-graduate work could be expected to score higher than a 20-year-old person who had proceeded no further than high school. The cultural implications of this fact are important, for if the decline in test score with age is least noticeable in those groups given the most education and most marked in those given the least, this surely is some evidence of the existence of school and cultural influences on intelligence test results.

Variation within the Individual

The scores of intelligence tests are also unsatisfactory when a person shows any marked degree of asymmetry in his mental development. The point has been referred to on page 64 in connection with Kent's suggestion that intelligence tests should be given as batteries rather than as scales—batteries composed of independently standardised units, so that each person may be tested on those units which are most appropriate to his particular case. A single score represented by the I.Q. does not indicate whether the person being tested is equally backward or normal or superior in every respect, or whether he shows wide variability in his performance of the different tasks in the scale. The same I.Q. for two individuals may represent entirely different types of mentality. In fact, of course, the competent clinical psychologist takes account of this in his report which is of greater diagnostic importance for the descriptive material it contains than for its I.Q. This being so there is a strong argument in favour of adopting some such scheme as Kent has suggested so that the report may be made more objective than is at present possible, for the present tests of intelligence do not usually contain a sufficient variety of items to make it possible to bring out this point adequately, for, as has already been pointed out, most of them up to quite recent times have been heavily overloaded with verbal items.

In some cases the asymmetry in mental development is of considerable proportions. Occasionally, among the feeble-minded, one encounters individuals who are termed *idiots savants* (though the term is a misnomer, for they are usually neither idiots nor geniuses), individuals who display a striking ability in calculation, musical ability, mechanical aptitude, drawing, memory and so on. The one field in which they do not seem to be found is in verbal aptitude. This is perhaps not so surprising as it sounds, for most intelligence tests, as we have seen, have a verbal basis so that an individual being tested by them would not appear as feeble-minded. And, similarly, since language enters into the practical affairs of our culture to such a considerable degree, a person who is linguistically proficient may be more easily able to compensate for deficiencies in other respects than someone whose asymmetrical development has proceeded along other lines. Consequently, the verbally proficient are not so likely to find their way into institutions for the feeble-minded as are those who are proficient in other directions.

Cases have been reported from institutions for the feeble-minded of inmates who possess phenomenal powers of memory, of people who can give the essential facts about any prominent character in history, including the most important dates in his life. Much of this knowledge is acquired by a concentration of interest along this particular line, through making detailed studies of all the available historical and biographical books. But that it is not all of a purely rote form is indicated by the answers that such a person may give when further questions are put to him about the material—that is to say he can often organise, systematise and synthesise his material : he is not always put out of his stride if he is interrupted in the middle of what he is saying, and his material is not necessarily of the mechanical, parrot-like form such as is found in some official guides (who are not inmates of institutions for the feeble-minded).

Cases of " lightning calculators " and of arithmetical prodigies among the feeble-minded have also been reported. One, on being asked how many seconds a man had lived who was 70 years 17 days and 12 hours old, gave the answer after $1\frac{1}{2}$ minutes as 2,210,500,800 seconds. One of his questioners worked it out with paper and pencil and came to a different answer, whereupon the lightning calculator informed him that he had forgotten to allow for leap years.

One of the most famous cases is that of J. H. Pullen who died

at the age of 66 in 1916 in Earlswood Institution.[1] Pullen's linguistic development was probably hampered by the fact that he was very deaf. At any rate he could not talk until he was seven years old, and for a long time only uttered the word " muvver ". He never went to school as no school would take him. He was able to wash and dress and take care of his person, and to write and spell the names of simple objects, but this was about as far as he could go in that direction. Nevertheless, he showed a very remarkable proficiency in mechanical construction, in drawing and in modelling. He spent $3\frac{1}{4}$ years making a model of a steamship 10 ft. long which was fastened together by nearly $1\frac{1}{4}$ million wooden pins and more than 5,500 copper rivets. It possessed thirteen perfectly finished models of lifeboats which could be raised and lowered on davits. It was fitted with engines, copper paddles, brass anchors and a screw, and it contained state cabins decorated and furnished with chairs, tables, beds and bunks. The model was based on drawings which he made himself, and many of the parts were manufactured with special tools which he himself designed. Another of his models was a robot 13 ft. high which could raise its arms, move its head, open and shut its mouth and eyes and protrude its tongue.

Such cases are, however, extremes. They are mentioned in order to illustrate how misleading a picture can be which is based on a score in an intelligence test without a discussion of the different aspects of development. In most cases the different aspects of behaviour show a more equal level of development, and for these an I.Q. grading is of more practical advantage, provided that it is combined with a discussion of any special abilities or disabilities an individual may possess.

Different authorities have suggested slightly different I.Q. levels for the different grades, and they have estimated rather different percentages of the population in the different levels.

Thus Cattell [2] suggests the classification shown in Table II.

In their standardisation of the New Stanford Revision of the Binet-Simon scale Terman and Merrill [3] obtained the approximate frequencies at different levels shown in Table III.

From these figures it will be seen that some latitude must be allowed when the diagnosis is made by means of intelligence tests. The various groupings are somewhat arbitrary. In practice the actual diagnosis, so far as those of subnormal intelli-

---

[1] Tredgold (18). [2] Cattell (4).
[3] From Terman and Merrill (17), p. 37.

TABLE II

Grading.	I.Q.	Frequency in Population.
Genius or near genius	170 and over	0·2 per cent.
Very brilliant	160–170	0·3 ,,
Brilliant	150–160	0·6 ,,
Very superior	140–150	1·4 ,,
Superior	130–140	3·5 ,,
Very bright	120–130	9·0 ,,
Bright	110–120	15·0 ,,
(Superior) average	100–110	20·0 ,,
(Inferior) average	90–100	20·0 ,,
Dull	80–90	15·0 ,,
Subculturally dull	70–80	9·0 ,,
Borderline mentally defective	65–70	2·2 ,,
Mentally defective :		
1. Feeble-minded [1]	45–65	3·1 ,,
2. Imbecile	25–45	0·6 ,,
3. Idiot	25 and below	0·1 ,,

TABLE III

I.Q.	Frequency.
35–44	0·25 per cent.
45–54	0·25 ,,
55–64	1·5 ,,
65–74	3·5 ,,
75–84	9·0 ,,
85–94	19·5 ,,
95–104	24·0 ,,
105–114	21·5 ,,
115–124	12·5 ,,
125–134	5·5 ,,
135–144	2·0 ,,
145–154	0·3 ,,
155–164	0·1 ,,

gence are concerned, turns in this country on behavioural and social criteria rather than on test results. Those regarded as suffering from mental defect are those who possess a deficiency in the kind of abilities which are necessary in order to survive in the cultural pattern of our society. If they happen to possess deficiencies in the ability to draw or to appreciate art or to understand the working of machines they may still be regarded as intellectually normal. From the point of view of diagnosis it is the *social* criteria that matter. So, *idiots* are those who are so

[1] The term *moron* is the equivalent in the United States of the term *feeble-minded* in England.

defective in mental ability that they are unable to guard themselves against common physical dangers ; *imbeciles* are those who
by reason of mental defect existing from birth or from an early
age are incapable of earning their own living, but are capable of
guarding themselves against common physical dangers : *feeble-
minded* persons are those who are capable of earning a living
under favourable circumstances, but who are incapable from
mental defect existing from birth or from an early age (*a*) of
competing on equal terms with their normal fellows, (*b*) of managing their own affairs or themselves with ordinary prudence.

Apart from a certain number of clinical types of organic
amentia the feeble-minded are not clearly differentiable from the
normal in physical characteristics.

GENIUS

At the other end of the scale there is again a certain arbitrari-
ness about the classification of those who are regarded as being
of the genius or near-genius level. Both time and the man are
necessary in order for genius to appear. The right man at the
wrong time or the wrong man at the right time fail to achieve
that permanence of distinction and eminence which is the right
of the true genius. It is almost certain that there must have been
many men who in other times, in other societies, or with other
environmental opportunities would have been acclaimed as
geniuses, and have retained the title of genius through the genera-
tions. Similarly men have often been acclaimed as geniuses by
their own times and people although they have passed into
obscurity a generation later.

In some societies or in some periods pathological traits have
rendered a man acclaimed as a genius, and it may be argued
that *any* genius is bound to be pathological in the sense of being
at the extreme range of ability. Ability is undoubtedly necessary
before a man can be a genius, but perhaps other qualities like an
active imagination, an orderly and accessible memory and a
very strong interest in a particular line of activity are necessary
too. Nevertheless, the characteristics which a society will look
for in its geniuses will partly depend on the particular values to
which that society attaches especial importance. Thus, within
our own cultural pattern at the present time, it is usual to regard
the linguistic and more abstract abilities as " higher " than the
more practical kinds of ability. Academic work is generally considered to be " higher " than managerial work in business and

considerably higher than precision work in factories. Thus Francis Galton's letter [1] to his sister the day before his fifth birthday is regarded by us as the work of an early genius :

MY DEAR ADÈLE,
I am four years old and I can read any English book. I can say all the Latin substantives and adjectives and active verbs besides 52 lines of Latin poetry. I can cast up any sum in addition and can multiply by 2, 3, 4, 5, 6, 7, 8, [9], 10, [11].
I can also say the pence table. I read French a little and I know the clock.

FRANCIS GALTON
Febuary 15 1827

The only misspelling is in the word " February ". The numbers 9 and 11 are bracketed because one had been scratched out with a knife and the other was covered by a bit of paper pasted over it.

From a technical point of view people are sometimes classified as of genius level when their I.Q. exceeds 140, and a fair amount of work has been undertaken on this basis within recent years.[2] This level is regarded by other authorities as being too low. Whatever the level, however, such a classification turns on the abstract and usually linguistic qualities implicit in intelligence tests that have already been discussed. It might be preferable to approach the question rather from the point of view of searching for different types of genius, even though this might mean that an accurate quantitative classification was not possible. If this approach had been made it is possible that men like J. H. Pullen would have been classified among the geniuses rather than among the mental defectives. The whole question, however, needs a great deal more consideration than it has been given up to now. The amount of work on genius is very small in comparison with that undertaken into the different types of mental defect.

REFERENCES

1. ARTHUR, G., *A Point Scale of Performance Tests*. New York : Commonwealth Fund, 1930, pp. 82.
2. BINET, A., and SIMON, TH., " Sur la nécessité d'établir un diagnostic scientifique des états inférieurs de l'intelligence ". *L'Année psychologique*, 1905, 11, 163–244.
3. BURT, C., *Mental and Scholastic Tests*. London : King, 1922, pp. 432.

[1] See Morgan (12), p. 329.
[2] The question of the inheritance of ability is discussed in my forthcoming book, *The Framework of Human Behaviour*.

4. CATTELL, R. B., *General Psychology*. Cambridge, Mass. : Sci-Art., 1941, pp. 624.

5. DREVER, J., and COLLINS, M., *Performance Tests of Intelligence*. Edinburgh : Oliver & Boyd, 1936, pp. 56.

6. HAMLEY, H. R., *The Testing of Intelligence*. London : Evans, 1935, pp. 175.

7. HOLLINGWORTH, L. S., *Children above 180 I.Q.* London : Harrap, 1942, pp. 332.

8. KENT, G. H., " Suggestions for the Next Revision of the Binet-Simon Scale ", *Psychol. Record*, 1937, 1, 407–34.

9. KNIGHT, R., *Intelligence and Intelligence Tests*. London : Methuen, 1933, pp. 98.

10. LEITER, R. G., " The Leiter International Performance Scale ". *Univ. Hawaii Bull.*, 1936, 15, 1–42.

11. MILES, C. C., and MILES, W. R., " The Correlation of Intelligence Scores and Chronological Age from Early to Late Maturity ". *Amer. J. Psychol.*, 1932, 48, 44–78.

12. MORGAN, J. J. B., *The Psychology of Abnormal People*. London : Longmans, Green, 1928, pp. 627.

13. PENROSE, L. S., and RAVEN, J. C., " A New Series of Perceptual Tests : Preliminary Communication ". *Brit. J. Psychol. (Med. Sect.)*, 1936, 16, 97–104.

14. PINTER, R., and PATERSON, R., *A Scale of Performance Tests*. New York : Appleton, 1917, pp. 218.

15. SPEARMAN, C. E., " ' General Intelligence ' objectively determined and measured." *Amer. J. Psychol.*, 1904, 15, 201–93.

16. TERMAN, L. M., *Genetic Studies of Genius*. London : Harrap, 1926–30. 3 vols.

17. ——, and MERRILL, M.A., *Measuring Intelligence*. London : Harrap, 1937, pp. 461.

18. TREDGOLD, A. F., *Mental Deficiency*. London : Baillière, Tyndall & Cox, 1922, pp. 546.

19. WILLOUGHBY, R. R., " Family Similarities in Mental Abilities ". *Genet. Psychol. Monog.*, 1927, 2, 235–77.

20. WOODWORTH, R. S., *Psychology*. London : Methuen, 1940, 12th edn., pp. 632.

CHAPTER VI

THE ASSESSMENT OF
PERSONALITY, TEMPERAMENT AND TYPES

INTRODUCTORY

We have seen in Chapter V that many difficulties arise in the exact interpretation of intelligence test results. These difficulties are, however, light in comparison with those arising out of methods of gauging personality and temperament. Intelligence tests possess the advantage, such as it is, that they have been highly standardised and used on a very large number of people, and that much research has been undertaken to try to find out what it is that they are really measuring. But tests of personality and temperament are of more recent development, and even those psychologists who put most faith in tests are unwilling to regard them with the same degree of confidence that they extend to tests of intelligence.

Just as different approaches have been made to the study of intelligence, so too have different approaches been made to the study of temperament and personality. But whereas with intelligence nearly all the methods have concentrated on a high degree of quantification, the methods of measuring personality and temperament have ranged from the objectivity of the questionnaire and factor analysis, through the combination of objectivity and skilled interpretation to be found in the Rorschach method and the interview-cum-rating scale technique, to the much more qualitative approach employed by most typologies. We will consider each of these approaches in turn.[1]

THE QUESTIONNAIRE

The first difference between a questionnaire and a test that strikes one is that there is no personal contact in the questionnaire. One result of this is that there is a greater possibility for misunderstanding in the questionnaire situation, for provided that

---

[1] Since the beginning of the war many new ideas have been developed by those who have been engaged on the selection of personnel for the services. For security reasons this material has not so far been published. When it is possible for the originators to publish it together with their methods of validation, it will prove most interesting reading.

the test is not being given to a large group of people at the same time—and with some tests this is impossible—one can often notice the point at which the person being tested is puzzled or has misunderstood the situation, and can take precautions in future to clear up this possible source of misunderstanding. But in the questionnaire situation—unless the questionnaire is being given individually, in which case it loses a lot of its advantages— this is not possible, and even if a careful preliminary pilot survey has been made in order to eliminate as many sources of mis- understanding as possible, some frequently still remain. Then, the questionnaire is more dependent on a person's goodwill than is a test, for although no test result can be relied upon unless a person's full co-operation has been gained, it is easier to obtain this in a situation of personal contact than it is when the question- naire reaches a person by post at his home or office. This factor of goodwill may affect the relative accuracy of test and question- naire results in another way : it is easier to affect one's score by giving false reactions in a questionnaire than it is in a test situa- tion, for most tests are intended to find out what a person can do, while questionnaires in most cases are intended to find out what he has done or how he feels or thinks about different problems.

Nevertheless, in spite of these disadvantages, the question- naire has been widely used—particularly in the United States— for little labour appears to be rewarded by relatively quick returns. It should be remembered, too, that as the investigator using the questionnaire is usually more interested in group than in individual results, some of the difficulties that arise when the answers of any one individual are considered may disappear in the group results. As Vernon [1] remarks, the answers from people treating the questionnaire flippantly may be counter- balanced by the answers of those who are conscientious, and the same thing is true of the effect of temporary moods or chance experiences on the answers : the bias in the answers from those who are feeling over-optimistic or high-spirited may be cancelled by the answers from those who happen to be feeling more depressed than usual when they are doing the questionnaire. Only if a large proportion of the group is influenced in precisely the same way will the group results be seriously upset.

In view of the difficulties, however, it is usual to take a number of precautions when a questionnaire is drawn up.[2] It

[1] Vernon (33), p. 16.   [2] Idem (34), pp. 206-7.

has been shown, for example, that double-barrelled or two-clause questions ought to be avoided, because people tend to answer the first alternative : that the order in which questions are asked should be varied in a proportion of the questionnaires so as to avoid the bias caused by many people tending to answer the questions at the beginning of a line or column : that questions which suggest a conventionally acceptable alternative arouse less resentment, and will therefore be answered more frankly than the reverse, e.g. Vernon [1] points out that more people may be willing to answer " No " to, " Have you always declared the whole of your income to the Inland Revenue Commissioners ? " than will answer " Yes " to, " Have you ever defrauded the Inland Revenue Commissioners by omitting to declare part of your income ? " : that prejudice is more readily shown in immediate and personal situations than in remote and impersonal ones : [2] that questions which express one's own views are likely to be given more weight and treated more seriously than those which express the opposite : [3] that some types of question are more suggestive than others,[4] and so on. Furthermore, in order to guard against, and to be able to eliminate, the questions in which flippant replies or even a deliberate falsification of the answers have been given, a number of techniques may be employed.   If the questionnaire is long enough the same question can be asked in slightly different forms in different parts of the questionnaire, and the person's answers to the different questions may be compared : or "jokers ", that is to say questions which have nothing to do with the subject being investigated, may be introduced : [5] or again the apparent interpretation and the actual interpretation may be different : [6] or the questionnaire may be given a title that will make it appear to be testing some thing different from what it is in fact testing.[7]

But even if all these precautions have been taken it is still desirable to take some final steps before actually launching the questionnaire.

First, the investigator should " soak " himself in the field of his enquiry, and discuss it with many persons of divergent opinions, before he attempts to formulate his specific questions and answers. Secondly, the formulation should be undertaken by several persons, all familiar with the field, rather than by himself alone.

[1] Vernon (34), p. 206. [2] Watson (36).
[3] Ibid. [4] Muscio (37).
[5] Pressey (24). [6] Hartshorne and May (13).
[7] Terman and Miles (29).

G

Thirdly, the questionnaire should be tried out on a small group of persons, who may draw attention to ambiguities and difficulties, before it is distributed widely.[1]

Finally, a word needs to be said about the validity and reliability of a questionnaire. A questionnaire is valid if it measures what it sets out to measure ; it is reliable if respondents give substantially the same replies when the questionnaire is repeated. It is possible to have a questionnaire with high validity but low reliability, e.g. when a questionnaire at one moment accurately measures what it sets out to measure, but does not give the same results when repeated, because of a rapid fluctuation in the respondents' opinions ; or when the questions are truly representative of the quality being measured, but because there are not enough of them, or because the respondents deliberately falsify their answers, the results which emerge are not sufficiently detailed or accurate. It is also possible to have a questionnaire with high reliability but low validity, e.g. one which gives identical results on repetition, but results which are not a true indication of the characteristics it is intended to measure. Various techniques have been developed [2] so that an investigator may test both the reliability and the validity of his questionnaire before launching it on a large scale.

Types of Questionnaire

Out of the hundreds of questionnaires that have been devised we may mention four types to illustrate some of the different methods on which they have been based. As a result of the advances in psychiatry during the war of 1914-18 Woodworth drew up a paper and pencil questionnaire whose object was to diagnose the ability of men to adjust themselves to the strains of life in the Forces. The questionnaire was based on the symptoms which were actually found in men of the fighting forces who had broken down under the strain, gathered together and published by MacCurdy.[3] Woodworth's questionnaire has undergone many revisions. Some of the questions were intended to investigate attitudes rather than facts, e.g. an affirmative answer to the questions, " Do you think tobacco has harmed you ? " or " Do you have too many sexual dreams ? " together with other similar replies, would disclose the existence of anxieties. The latter question in particular has been subjected to much derision.

[1] Vernon (34), p. 207.   [2] See, for example, Vernon (33) and (34).
[3] MacCurdy (19).

" What ", it is often asked, " is too many ? " This, however, need not be answered, because the object of the question is to discover whether the person answering it thinks he has too many, irrespective of the actual number he has, and the same thing is true of the question about tobacco and others of a similar kind. One of the revisions of this questionnaire is called by Thurstone [1] " The Personality Schedule ". This contains forty-two questions of which the following are examples :

" 6. Are your feelings easily hurt ?

" 10. Do you worry over possible misfortunes ?

" 15. Do you get discouraged easily ?

" 34. Do you lack self-confidence ? "

In an attempt to measure the width of a person's emotional reactions Pressey [2] suggested a cross-out (x-o) test. Some people react emotionally to a wide range of objects and situations whereas others show little variation in feeling. Pressey put forward his questionnaire for research purposes, but it has been widely applied. In one section the respondent has to cross out any-thing· he thinks is wrong, e.g. " Begging, swearing, smoking, flirting, spitting " ; in another he has to cross out anything which makes him feel anxious or worried, e.g. " Sickness, enemies, money, blushing, failure " ; in another he has to cross out any word whose meaning is unpleasant, e.g. " Disgust, fear, sex, suspicion, aunt ". A total of 500 items are included.

A rather different technique is used in Allport's [3] Ascendance-Submission test. In this the respondents are presented with a number of situations such as they might have been in several times already in their lives, and they are asked to imagine how they would actually behave in those situations, for example :

> At church, a lecture, or an entertainment, if you arrive after the programme has commenced and find that there are people standing but also that there are front seats available which might be secured without " piggishness " but with considerable con-spicuousness, do you take the seats ?—
>
> Habitually . . . .
> Occasionally . . . .
> Never . . . .

Thurstone [4] has devised an elaborate technique for measuring a person's attitudes on about forty different topics, and he claims

[1] Thurstone (31). [2] Pressey (24).
[3] Allport (1). [4] Thurstone (30).

it gives a more exact indication of the person's attitudes than most other methods. First of all a large number of heterogeneous opinions about, say, the movies are collected from a wide variety of sources. These are then sorted by scores of judges into a number of piles which represent degrees of favourableness or unfavourableness of the attitude expressed by each statement, and from these it is possible to calculate the score (representing the degree of favourableness or unfavourableness) which should be attached to each statement, and to eliminate those which are unreliable. In the case of the attitude towards the movies the score ranged from 5 (the most favourable) to 0 (the most unfavourable). Favourable and unfavourable opinions balanced each other fairly evenly so that the middle score was about 2·5.

> (4·7) The movies are the most powerful influence for good in American life.
> (0·0) It is a sin to go to the movies.
> (2·4) Sometimes I feel that the movies are desirable and sometimes I doubt it.

The figures in brackets represent the degree of favourableness or unfavourableness of the statements. The respondent, without knowing the scores, marks the statements with which he is in agreement, thus indicating his average attitude and also the range of opinions with which he is willing to ally himself.

FACTOR ANALYSIS [1]

In the factorial technique a number of people (the larger the better) is given a battery of tests, and a table of correlation coefficients, representing the degree of agreement between the scores on the different tests is worked out. From this it may emerge that the scores on some of the tests are more highly correlated than those of others, and it may be possible to account for those showing the highest correlation by a general factor. Then, when the effect of this general factor on the correlation coefficients is removed, the remaining correlation coefficients are examined to discover whether a second factor can be extracted, and so on.

A number of factors are claimed to have been isolated by this technique, e.g. " v " a verbal factor, " $c+$ " or " surgency ", which Cattell [2] believes to be very similar to extraversion,

---

[1] See, for example, Burt (8), for an excellent and unprejudiced account of the advantages and limitations of factor analysis.
[2] Cattell (9), p. 149.

" *c* — " or " desurgency ", which is similar to introversion, " *p* " or " perseveration ", and so on.   Clearly it would be a great advantage if, instead of giving more or less adequate descriptions of a large number of different attitudes and functions and senti- ments of human beings, we were able to discover a few fundamental and basic elements, which, perhaps, might even turn out on further investigation to be intimately related to an individual's genetic constitution.   It would open the possibility of exciting experiments on the Mendelian inheritance of these factors.[1]

Unfortunately the statistical techniques which are employed to discover the existence of factors sometimes have the dis- advantage of producing a factor which is such a conglomeration of heterogeneous aspects of traits that it has little or no meaning in behavioural terms.   This is perhaps inevitable because of the techniques which have to be employed in order to isolate a factor. Very large numbers of people are given the tests, statistical formulæ are applied to the results and a number of factors are isolated.   Now what this means in fact is that these factors represent average tendencies, and there is no good reason for assuming that they represent anything in any one of the individuals who formed the original group.   Everyone's abilities are mixed with everyone else's when the statistical technique is employed, and everyone consequently loses his identity.   Some of the factors which emerge would, one would have thought, make the point sufficiently obvious to anyone who was not so convinced that his statistical techniques must give the right answer that he cannot see beyond them.   One factor, for example, contains the following peculiar combination of characteristics :

Rarely thinks about the meaning of life
Does not enjoy spicy and highly seasoned foods
Much interested at a play in whether the characters violate con- ventional codes of behaviour
Prefers working with people to working with things or materials
Considerably interested in politics
Day-dreaming has increased during the past five years
Differs considerably from intimate friends in interests, etc.[2]

How is it possible to give a name to such an assortment ? Factorial psychologists usually reply to this by using a single letter : *g, v, k, o, w, s, m, p, c,* etc., as if the use of an alphabet

---

[1] See my forthcoming book, *The Framework of Human Behaviour.*
[2] Example given by Vernon (33), p. 39.

soup of mathematical symbols excused them from defending behavioural concepts. What is worse is that the initial letter is often the first letter of an actual behavioural concept. Thus as soon as "p", for example, is understood to refer to "perseveration" we have passed from statistical analysis to qualitative interpretation, and yet it is so easy (as with "g") to fall into the pitfall of believing that what is true of the mathematical symbol is also true of the behavioural concept. For this no evidence exists. Nor can one see why the miscellaneous group of characteristics displayed by those with high or low "p" scores should indicate any degree of "perseveration" in the sense in which the word is used in less abnormal psychology. Cattell,[1] for instance, reports that a person who makes a low "p" score is, among other things, inclined to be nagging, restless and fussy, inconsiderate and tough, selfish and impetuous, interested in mechanical, scientific and mathematical matters and to have few dreams. While a person with a high "p" score is sceptical and pessimistic, conservative in his habits, sensitive, interested in history, languages and humanities, absent-minded, dreamy and sentimental, and slovenly in dress. Confusion rather than clarity would seem to have been added to the picture by calling "p" "perseveration". One can imagine that Humpty Dumpty would have paid a high price for this word or letter of the alphabet which has so many different and unexpected meanings.

Finally, the assumption that because two individuals get the same score on a test they possess the same characteristic is not necessarily true. We have already considered this point in connection with the testing of intelligence and it is likely to be still more pertinent in connection with personality or temperamental characteristics. As Vernon [2] points out, the organisation of the personalities of the two individuals may be entirely different, so that a certain amount of a characteristic in one personality organisation may mean something quite different from the same amount of that characteristic in another individual with a different type of personality organisation. " Attempts at measurement, whether with tests or with ratings, inevitably disrupt the personality into such separate bits as can be handled by our quantitative techniques, but they cannot put it together again." [3] Vernon adds,

Schematically expressed, statistics can examine the relationship between $a \times A + b \times B \ldots$ and $m \times M + n \times N \ldots$

[1] Cattell (9), p. 209.   [2] Vernon (32).   [3] Ibid., p. 2.

where A, B, M, etc., are psychological variables, a, b, m, etc. are their weights in a group of Subjects. But to examine the relationship of $aAbB$ . . . with $mMnN$ . . . in one Subject and of $a'Ab'B$ . . . $m'Mn'N$ . . . in another Subject, where $aAbB$ . . . etc., represent organised products, not aggregates, would seem to be outside the present scope of correlations.[1]

THE FREE ASSOCIATION METHOD

A method which employs a combination of objective presentation with some degree of subjective interpretation is the free association technique employed by Jung.[2]   One of the ways in which Jung used it was in the diagnosis of complexes in order to discover in what directions his patients were maladjusted. The person being tested is given a list of words to each of which he has to reply as quickly as he can with the first word that comes into his head.   The lists are usually long, as it is believed that the results are not reliable unless about 100 words are employed.   The complex indicators are mainly to be found in abnormally long or abnormally short reaction times, for example any response which takes more than $2\frac{1}{2}$ secs. to make ; the inability to make any response in a minute ; the repetition of the stimulus word ; an apparent misunderstanding of the stimulus word ; a response with the same reaction word to two or more different stimulus words ; a strange or apparently senseless reaction, and so on.

A somewhat different technique has been used by Kent and Rosanoff.[3]   They drew up their list in such a way as to try to avoid those words which might be specially liable to call up personal experiences, and they standardised it by tabulating the responses of 1,000 individuals to each of the stimulus words.   It was then possible to see with what percentage of frequency any given response word was made, and to classify the responses into various groups of common responses and various types of individual reactions—particularly those of a pathological nature. Then, when the test was used on new subjects it was possible to estimate the degree of individuality, conventionality and abnormality of their responses.   The list was, however, standardised in 1910 in the United States.   If it is to be used in this country in this way it would be advantageous to make a new standardisation.

[1] Vernon (32), p. 2, footnote.   It should be added that Vernon might dissociate himself from these views to-day, since he has recently somewhat changed his views on the value of factor analysis.
[2] Jung (16).
[3] Kent and Rosanoff (17).

THE RORSCHACH METHOD

An indirect measure of personality characteristics is the Rorschach ink blot test.[1] Its accurate interpretation depends to a large extent on the width of the tester's clinical experience of its use, although many aspects of the procedure are highly standardised and objectified. The test consists of ten bilaterally symmetrical ink blots which are shown one by one to the person being tested who is told to describe anything that they suggest to him. He may look at the blots in any position and for as long as he pleases. His responses are recorded and subsequently classified. The classifications include, (1) the type of stimulus selected—whether the blot as a whole, a detail, a rare detail and so on are reacted to, (2) the determinant and quality of the response—whether the blot or some part of the blot suggests an experience of felt movement ; whether colour was the sole determinant of the response ; whether colour was primary and form secondary, or form primary and colour secondary ; or whether form alone determined the response, and, if so, whether the form was good or poor, (3) the content of the response, including human and animal forms, human and animal details, common responses and original responses. Other observations are also made, e.g. the time taken before a response is made to a blot, and the total time taken over the ten blots, the degree of card turning, perseveration in responses, verbosity and elaboration, the general attitude to the experiment, and so on.

According to the relative proportions of the answers in different categories, as well as according to the absolute number in each category, an estimate is made of the respondent's type, e.g. creative, abstract, practical, analytical, organising. Healthy, superior adults, for instance, generally give more whole, movement and form responses than the average, but fewer colour and animal responses ; the feeble-minded usually give fewer whole, movement, colour and form, but more animal responses than the average. The more intelligent individual usually also gives responses that possess a wide range of meanings, whereas if there are too many animal responses, or any other single category, a degree of stereotypy is indicated. A high productivity of answers in the blots which contain colours is associated with affective release.

[1] See Beck (5) or Rorschach (26). The blots themselves are provided in Vol. 2 of Rorschach's book.

Nevertheless, all the categories are interdependent; for example, the responses involving movement are held to indicate mental creativity, but if the responses to the cards containing colour are poor relatively to those to the others, this indicates that the mental creativity shown by a relatively large number of movement responses is repressed. If, on the other hand, in the same person, the colour responses are relatively numerous, this will indicate that the mental creativity is being externalised and is finding release.[1] Thus the accurate interpretation of the various elements varies with the background of the personality in which they appear, and each element has to be interpreted in the light of all the others.

THE INTERVIEW

Most people consider themselves to be good interviewers, but when their powers in this respect are subjected to experimental investigation it is found that many of them are mistaken. Experiments on judging characteristics from photographs have always given disappointing results. The reason may be that such judgments are inevitably based on the essentially artificial abstraction of one momentary phase of a person's behaviour from the total series of acts which might enable us to describe his characteristics more accurately. Certainly it is true that studies of expressive behaviour such as have been performed by Allport and Vernon [2] and by Estes [3] have been more convincing.

In Estes' experiment a short film was made of a number of people whose traits of personality had been intensively studied for a period of a year by a group of psychologists. The film showed them engaged in various activities—wrestling, holding a lighted match as long as possible, building card houses, and a few others. They were then rated by a group of psychiatric social workers, all of whom had had at least two years' practical experience, on the same characteristics as had been studied by the psychologists during the previous year. The object, therefore, was to compare impressions which could be gained while watching a two-minute film with the results of a long-term experimental and clinical study. The experiment indicated quite clearly that in such a situation the accuracy of the judgment depended on three factors—the nature of the characteristics that were being measured, the character of the person being judged, and the ability of the person making the judgment.

[1] Earl (10), pp. 252-3.   [2] Allport and Vernon (3).   [3] Estes (11).

So far as the characteristics themselves were concerned, overt and expressive traits like aggressiveness and submissiveness, apathy and intensity, and inhibition or impulsiveness, were more accurately rated than were characteristics like snobbishness, and realism or paranoia. So far as the people being judged were concerned, all the raters—good and poor alike—found much the same relative difficulty in judging the different candidates : and so far as the inherent shrewdness of the judge himself was concerned, the average correctness of the ten best judges was 33 per cent. better than that of the ten poorest, the record of the best single judge being 62 per cent. better than that of the worst.

An elaborate analysis of the qualifications required by a good judge of other people has been made by Allport.[1] He maintains that people on the whole are more likely to judge accurately those who most closely resemble themselves. The best judge of a characteristic is one who possesses that characteristic himself, and a man is a better judge of another man than he is of a woman. Closely related to this is the need for maturity and for an experience of human nature in its most varied forms, for the wider and more varied one's experiences, the more likely is one to have actually performed oneself a type of reaction one observes in someone else. Contrary to popular belief, therefore, youth is more likely to misjudge its elders than they are to return the compliment. It follows from this also that the better the judge the more complex and subtle is his personality likely to be. The second group of desirable qualities are insight and detachment. The better one appreciates one's own failings, follies and hypocrisies, the less is one likely to make a superficial diagnosis of other people. The greater one's insight the more introspective and introverted one is likely to be also, and this in its turn implies a resistance to the changing influences of different environments and a reasonable detachment from them. The third group of qualities concerns intelligence : the good judge must be able to see the relation between a person's present activity and the unseen background out of which it has emerged. He must be able to reconstruct a person's characteristics from the few fragments which appear in an interview. In order to encourage and to nurture by patient questioning and a constant appearance of friendly interest the greatest possible frankness from the person interviewed, the good judge must possess in addition the gift of " social intelligence ".

[1] Allport (2), pp. 513–16.

Having discussed some of the characteristics required by a person if he is to make a satisfactory interviewer, it will be well to consider the precautions that must be taken to guard against the influence of bias and prejudice, and to establish the interview itself on a reasonable setting. The fact that the interview is an individual affair involving in its essence the element of human contact is both one of its main advantages and one of its main disadvantages when compared, say, with the questionnaire. It is disadvantageous in that when people may be dealt with only individually the amount of time required to investigate a group is very large. It is advantageous in that where there is individual human contact there is the possibility of developing a sufficiently flexible technique in the wording of questions, and in the order of presentation of topics, to get the most out of each individual who is investigated, instead of a vaguely moderate amount from everybody.

One further disadvantage of the interview technique compared with the questionnaire technique requires discussion. Although misconceptions about the meaning of questions may be more easily disposed of when the questions are presented in the course of the conversation that develops in the interview situation, yet at the same time it is far easier to convey suggestion by the spoken than by the written word. Not only may suggestion be conveyed by the actual form of words which is used in framing the question —a type of suggestion which may be conveyed equally well by the questionnaire, as we have already mentioned—but also by the way in which those words are spoken, by the relative emphasis that is laid upon them, and even by the speed or rhythm with which they are spoken.

It is extremely easy, therefore, for an interviewer's personal bias to influence the type of question he may ask or the way in which he asks it, so that the replies are not representative of the candidate's true views. The effect of such bias has been experimentally induced by Harvey [1] who gave her interviewers a character sketch of each candidate which suggested that the candidate was inferior in respect of one of three character traits—reliability, sociability or emotional stability. Without the interviewers' knowing it the bias did in fact adversely affect about 40 per cent. of the ratings they gave to the candidates on the critical traits. There was, however, a limit to the extent of the experimentally induced bias, and it was not sufficient to outweigh all the other

[1] Harvey (14).

clues from a person's appearance and behaviour that emerged in the course of the interview.

The effect of the personal bias of an interviewer on his reaction to the candidate often goes by the name of the " halo " effect, and it has become one of the principal things that all interviewers are repeatedly warned against.   Briefly, the halo effect is the tendency of interviewers who are personally attracted to a particular candidate to over-estimate the extent to which he possesses desirable characteristics, and to under-estimate him on undesirable characteristics.   Similarly, if an interviewer is faced with a candidate whom he finds irritating or repellent, he will tend to under-value his desirable characteristics and to overstress his undesirable. It is sometimes said that the halo effect does not matter very much if the purpose of an interview is to select a personal assistant for oneself, because it is pleasanter to work with someone whose personality one finds attractive, even though he may be somewhat inferior in other respects to a candidate who is personally less pleasing.   When, however, one is choosing a candidate to work with someone else one must be on one's guard against the halo effect much more, for one cannot be sure that a person who is pleasing to oneself will also prove pleasing to someone else. The truth of this will clearly depend on how far one's own idea of a pleasing person is shared by other people, how far, that is to say, one's own stereotype is common property.   Some stereotypes are certainly less widely shared than others : some people maintain that a green-eyed person is more trustworthy than a brown-eyed ; others believe the reverse to be true : some people think that red-haired individuals are quick-tempered : some think that a person who is neatly dressed will do his work neatly : some think that a person who talks quickly has a quick mind : and if a photograph is taken of a smiling candidate he will be rated more highly for intelligence than if he appears without a smile.   Certainly the idea of a pleasant personality is likely to be a stereotype that is fairly widely shared.

How, then, can one guard against the halo effect and the acceptance of stereotypes ?   This is where Allport's characteristics of the good judge of other people are useful—particularly the characteristics under the heading of insight and detachment.   The more one appreciates and is consciously aware of one's own bias, the less is one likely to rely on the stereotypes based upon them.[1]

[1] The halo effect has for some time been one of the principal things that all those who are engaged in interviewing have been warned against. So much have people

Finally, an interviewer's personal bias is likely to diminish in importance if he presents his character study to a small group of other skilled interviewers, and embodies their views in his final assessment of the candidate ; for then either his own bias will tend to cancel an opposing bias in some other member of the group, or else, if his bias is a generally accepted stereotype, some other member of the group may point to its existence if he fails to notice it himself.[1]

RATING SCALES

Among other techniques for controlling the influence of the halo effect, and so making the interview more objective, the application of a rating scale is often found to be useful.   Out of the many techniques which have been devised [2] we shall select only one or two for discussion.   One of the simplest is the ranking method.   This method is, however, only applicable in special conditions which usually do not exist in the interview situation. It is sometimes useful in the class-room where it is found that a teacher can more easily rank her pupils in order of intelligence from the lowest to the highest than make an estimate of the *amount* of intelligence that each possesses.

A different technique, which endeavours to be more quantitative, is to give numerical ratings.   In these the raters are given scales ranging from 0 to 5, or from 0 to 7, or from − 3 to + 3, etc.   They have to rate the amount of the quality that each person possesses by giving him one of these scores.   Usually raters have to be given careful instructions to see that they produce a more or less normal curve of error from the group they are rating : thus in every hundred ten should be + 2, twenty + 1, forty 0, twenty − 1 and ten should be − 2, or, if seven classes are used, in every hundred one or two should be + 3, ten should be + 2, twenty-three or twenty-four + 1, thirty should be 0, and so on.   However, if this technique is employed there is a danger that the rater will feel *forced* into making his categories fit the expected frequencies, and so the resulting picture will be to some extent inaccurate.

One of the difficulties with ratings is that different people's

been warned against it that there may now be a danger that some interviewers will over-compensate for it.   It is important, therefore, to be on one's guard against this, and to try to strike a balance between the halo and the over-compensated halo.
[1] For a discussion of the techniques which it is advisable to adopt in the interview itself, see Oldfield (23), Rodger (25), pp. 262-8, and Clement Brown (7), pp. 389-96.
[2] See Symonds (28), pp. 41-121, or Vernon (33), pp. 43-65.

standards differ. What one may consider a given degree of the characteristic being rated to be high another may consider to be only average or even low. In order to avoid this difficulty graphic rating scales are sometimes used. Different degrees of the quality are described in verbal terms by the use of descriptive adjectives. The rater marks the position on the scale that he thinks the person to be rated reaches. The ratings may subsequently be converted into quantitative scores, if it is desired to do so. By way of illustrating this technique the following is one of the items for " personal care " from a scale which Vernon [1] suggests for use in interviews :

Fastidious in dress	Good taste, neat, clean	Passable and inconspicuous	Careless in dress and cleanliness	Slovenly and unkempt

The choice of adjectives to describe the behaviour is important. Where possible, concrete definitions of behaviour should be given, and the use of neutral terms is desirable. Furthermore, Vernon [2] points out that most people avoid the use of the extreme degrees in their judgments and tend to put far too many people above the average on any desirable trait and too few below. This tendency may be overcome to some extent by a careful wording of the classes. Thus a more symmetrical distribution is obtained from

Poor	Fair	Good	Very good	Excellent

than from

Bad	Poor	Average	Good	Excellent

Finally, let us consider the question of the fineness of discrimination of ratings. The qualitative methods, e.g. ranking, possess the advantage over the quantitative methods that the degree of discrimination may be as fine as is desired. However, in practice, if the number of people ranked is large, a degree of artificiality is introduced into the rankings. For although the extreme individuals at both ends of the scale may stand out, yet there will be a crowd of average people in the middle who are not sufficiently different from one another to be able to be accurately ranked in order. The person ranking them will be

[1] Vernon (33), p. 57.   [2] Ibid., p. 46.

obliged to make false comparisons between them. In rating scales, too, the question of the fineness of discrimination is important. If the scale is too coarse the ratings will be unreliable because there will not be enough grades into which everyone can be fitted. On the other hand, if the scale is too fine the ratings will be unreliable because the rater may become exhausted while looking for minor degrees of difference between the individuals he is rating. Symonds [1] suggests that about seven grades is on the whole most satisfactory, although in practice five are more generally employed.

PHYSIQUE AND TEMPERAMENT

The possible association between physique and temperament has for a long time been a matter on which much speculation has existed. Hippocrates believed that people could be divided into two types according to the relative proportions of the " elements ", fire and water, in their make-up. Galen divided people into the four well-known types : sanguine, choleric, phlegmatic and melancholic, believing that these had a physical basis. The sanguine temperament, he believed, was caused by an excessive production of red blood cells by the marrow, and its psychological concomitants were optimism and cheerfulness. The choleric was due to an excess of yellow bile, and its psychological characteristics were hot temper and violence. The phlegmatic was due to an excess of phlegm, and the people who possessed this were cold and lethargic. The melancholic suffered from an excessive production of black bile liberated by the liver, and this caused them to be pessimistic and melancholy.

As the knowledge of the glands of internal secretion has developed a changing emphasis has been put on these theories. Nowadays it is more usual to regard the relationship between substances liberated into the blood-stream and behavioural characteristics in something like the following way :

(1) Excess of secretion from the thyroid gland leads a person to be excitable and active and to have all his movements speeded up. Physically the hyperthyroid individual is thin, while those with a deficiency of thyroid secretion (the hypothyroid) tend to be fat.

(2) Excess of secretion from the adrenal glands also has a stimulating effect. It is secretion from these glands that accompanies any strong emotion like rage or fear or pain, and it serves

[1] Symonds (28), p. 79.

the useful purpose of bracing the individual to meet the situation with more energy, intensity and duration.

(3) The pituitary produces two main secretions, one from the anterior and the other from the posterior lobe. Deficiency in the secretion from the anterior lobe leads to depression, lack of appetite and loss of sexual drive. Deficiency in the secretion from the posterior lobe leads to a general condition of fatness and dullness resembling hypothyroidism, together with a lack of mental stamina and ambition.

It will be seen from this that excess or deficiency of secretion from the glands of internal secretion seems to be associated more with the liberation of nervous energy than with anything else. There is a considerable degree of interaction between the different glands. Thus the pituitary acts as a spur for both the thyroid and the adrenal glands, and so on with the others. Besides, only in extreme cases of dysfunction are there likely to be marked alterations of personality, and within the normal range of the functioning of the glands other influences due to environment, habit formation and training are likely to be of more importance to the development of personality traits.

It still remains possible, however, that even within the normal range of glandular secretion there is an *indirect* relation between physical constitution and personality traits.[1] Over- or under-secretion from particular glands may make a person more or less active, and more or less physically attractive. Then, those whose good fortune it is to possess strong, healthy and attractive physical characteristics, together with a certain liveliness as a result of the glandular secretions, may find that they receive more social approval and are more readily accepted and drawn into different groups than are those who are weak, unattractive and slow. Thus the former may, as a result of their more ready acceptance, develop more social graces than the latter, and, as a result of this, be even more readily accepted by new groups. So a small difference in behaviour and appearance to begin with may, as a result of social forces, be developed into a bigger difference later on.

A second line in the development of the study of the relationship between temperament and personality began with the work on phrenology. The assumption underlying this work was that the mind could be split up into faculties and that these faculties were located in different parts of the head. Modern views do

[1] Allport (2), pp. 77–8.

not make it possible to accept either of these contentions. But even if they were true, the further requirement of the practical phrenologist that an excess or deficiency of any of these faculties causes a bump or depression in a certain part of the outside of the skull, is not in fact met. For it to be true, the outside of the skull would have to conform exactly to the inside, and also to the brain—whereas in fact the skull varies in thickness in different parts in different people. Consequently a bump or depression may be due to an extra thick or extra thin piece of skull just as much as to an excess or deficiency or philoprogenitiveness, amativeness, acquisitiveness, etc.

KRETSCHMER'S TYPES

Phrenology did, however, call attention to a possible relation between temperament and bodily structure—as distinct from glandular secretions—and this line of investigation has been taken up and developed to a high level by the work of Kretschmer.[1] As a result of a wide clinical experience Kretschmer came to the conclusion that there was a relationship between certain types of bodily physique and certain types of mental disorder. He then extended the concept of a correspondence between them to more normal temperamental differences. Kretschmer admitted that his types were ideals and that individuals might diverge from the ideal to a greater or lesser extent. But he pointed out that exactly the same thing was true in medicine. Cases of measles or chicken-pox very rarely show *all* the textbook symptoms, yet no one doubts the diagnosis on that account. Kretschmer found that patients suffering from the mental disorder known as manic-depression (in which there is a smooth variation in mood varying from exaltation to depression, combined with a ready response to changing stimuli) tended to be of pyknik bodily type—a type of physique characterised by its tendency to run to fat, its medium height, rounded figure, soft broad face and massive neck. He also found that patients suffering from schizophrenia (in which there is often a sudden jerky change in mood from hypersensitivity and excitability to frigidity and inaccessibility and in which the patients are often in poor contact with their environment) tended to be either of leptosomatic (tall and angular bodily type) ; or of athletic bodily type with well-developed shoulders and chest, tapering trunk and firm stomach ; or of dysplastic bodily type showing some marked abnormalities of

[1] Kretschmer (18).

physical development. He further maintained that in normal behaviour similar relationships were found. He divided normal individuals into cyclothymes and schizothymes on the basis of their temperamental characteristics—the two categories corresponding with the abnormal states of manic-depression or schizophrenia—and held that cyclothymes tended to be of pyknik bodily type, schizothymes of the other three bodily types.

Kretschmer gave short descriptions of a few typical cases of cyclothymes, e.g. the gay chatterbox, the quiet humorist, the silent good-tempered man, the happy enjoyers of life, and the energetic, practical man ; and of schizothymes, e.g. the polite, sensitive man, the world-hostile idealist, the cold, masterful natures and egoists, and the dried and emotionally lame.

The theory crystallises and tries to put on an experimental footing the traditional view expressed in literature and in the belief of the man in the street about the temperamental characteristics associated with roundness and adiposity on the one hand, or with leanness and angularity on the other. It is also the view of many clinical workers that the theory expresses a relationship that is frequently found in practice. Nevertheless, a certain degree of caution is necessary before accepting the theory. Not all investigations have ensured that the two groups are of the same age. Manic-depression is a disorder which is likely to occur at a later age than schizophrenia, so the average age of manic-depressives is likely to be higher than that of schizophrenics. Unless the age factor is controlled, therefore, any correlation between physique and temperament may be a spurious one due to the ordinary tendency of people to become better covered with flesh as they get older. In fact when the age factor is controlled the correlations are often reduced to negligible proportions. For instance Garvey [1] found that in a group of 130 manic-depressive and 130 schizophrenic patients closely matched for age there was an almost complete overlapping of the two groups in the different and extensive physical measurements and ratios that were computed. Not only were the averages of the two groups very similar, but also the range and the general form of the distribution were practically identical.

Jung's Typology

A different approach to the question of types has been to concentrate on the psychological aspects rather than to try to

[1] Garvey (12).

link them up with physical characteristics. One of the best known of these is Jung's division of people into introverts and extraverts.[1] Jung believed that these characteristics are innately determined. The introvert is a shy and impenetrable person whose attitude towards objects in the external world is characterised by his acting as if they were continually attempting to overpower him and had to be frustrated. The extravert is an open and sociable person whose attitude towards objects in the external world is characterised by his plasticity in adjusting to meet the changing circumstances in which he finds himself. The extravert will join in general applause given to a popular cause, the introvert will hold that merely because a cause is given temporary popularity that is not sufficient reason for believing it to be a good cause. The introvert tries to select out of the things going on around him those that fit in with his own mental make-up ; the extravert changes his interests in conformity with the changing events in the outside world.

In addition to these two general attitudes, Jung held that there were also four ways by which the attitude could express itself. These are known as thinking, feeling, sensation and intuition. For instance, the extravert thinking type collects facts for their own sake : the introvert thinking type collects them in an analytic spirit and as evidence to prove a theory. The extravert feeling type is a follower of fashion : the introvert feeling type has hidden depths of emotion under an impassive exterior. The extravert sensation type is realistic, and indulges in concrete enjoyment : the introvert sensation type takes his pleasures in his own way. The extravert intuition type is guided by practical possibilities and is the type that makes the successful merchant, speculator or politician : the introvert intuition type chases after ideals. He is a voice crying in the wilderness, and he is the type that becomes the prophet or the mystical dreamer.

In a still further addition to his theory Jung held that the thinking, feeling, sensation and intuition function types do not always express themselves in a pure form. Certain combinations are also possible, and thinking or feeling may be combined with either sensation or intuition.

Thus from his original division of people into two types Jung expanded his types into eight and subsequently into sixteen. But clearly the larger the number of types that has to be devised in order to cover the marginal individuals who do not

[1] Jung (16).

fit very obviously into the wider categories, the less becomes its value as a typological scheme. Furthermore, Jung tends to regard introversion and extraversion as qualitatively different forms of behaviour. For instance, the typical form of maladjustment of the introvert is entirely different from the typical form of maladjustment of the extravert. If this were so then a statistical analysis of introversion and extraversion would be expected to produce a " bi-modal " curve of something like the form shown in Fig. 17.

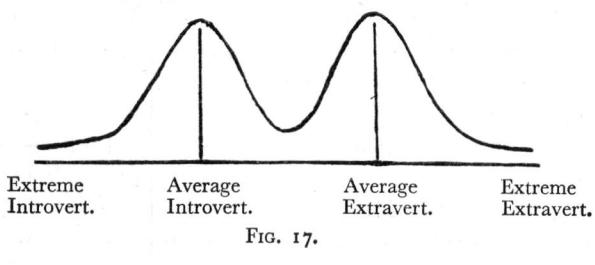

| Extreme Introvert. | Average Introvert. | Average Extravert. | Extreme Extravert. |

FIG. 17.

Most people here are either averagely introvert or averagely extravert, and fewer and fewer show a greater or smaller degree of extraversion or of introversion than the average. In fact, however, when questionnaires such as those of Neymann and Kohlstedt [1] or Heidbreder,[2] based on the characteristics which introverts and extraverts are supposed to show, are given to a large group of people, a curve of the normal unimodal type is usually obtained, with most people showing " ambiversion ", while fewer and fewer people are found as the degree of deviation from this average (towards either extreme extraversion or towards extreme introversion) increases (See Fig. 18).

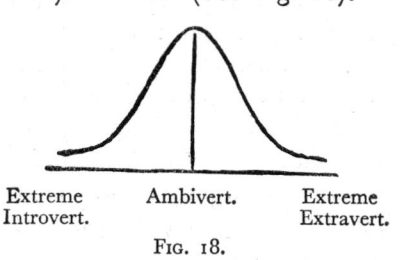

| Extreme Introvert. | Ambivert. | Extreme Extravert. |

FIG. 18.

Nevertheless the concept of introversion and extraversion has enjoyed a wide and popular appeal. It has even been applied by McDougall [3] to racial groups. Thus McDougall regards the

[1] Neymann and Kohlstedt (22).   [2] Heidbreder (15).
[3] McDougall (20), pp. 108-10.

Nordic as predominantly introvert whereas the Mediterraneans are predominantly extravert. In support of his hypothesis McDougall points to suicide rates. He illustrates this by discussing the typical reaction of the extravert and of the introvert on learning that his wife has run off with somebody else. If he is an extravert his anger will be directed against his rival, and he will tend to commit murder : if he is an introvert his sorrow will be turned inwards and he will tend to commit suicide. Certainly some of the figures for suicides support McDougall's hypothesis, and the figures that he himself uses are certainly impressive, the number of suicides in Denmark, Scandinavia, England and Australia being many times those in Ireland, Spain and Italy. However, when figures from other countries are included there is no such racial difference, for example, Scotland, which does not enter into McDougall's figures, has one of the lowest suicide rates in the whole of Europe. Furthermore, when figures for suicides in the same country at different times are compared, it is found that the rates vary very considerably, a country which had a relatively high rate at one time having a relatively low rate at another and *vice versa*.

SPRANGER'S TYPES

Another theory of types put forward by Spranger [1] is also based on attitudes. The six attitudes are theoretical, economic, æsthetic, social, political, and religious.

The theoretical attitude is characterised by objectivity. It leads to analysis and synthesis, to reasoning and to systematisation. Things are not recognised as beautiful or ugly, useful or useless, good or bad, but only as true or false. A man with this attitude is mainly interested in the discovery of truth. In his social relations he is an individualist, for his objective mental attitude does not find sympathetic support from other people, and he tends to regard family ties as relatively unimportant.

The economic attitude is guided by utility. A man with this attitude economises goods and forces, time and space in order to gain the maximum useful effect for himself. He is content to let beautiful landscapes be destroyed for economic motives, for he is interested in what is useful rather than in what is beautiful. He is thoroughly practical. He is also unsocial. He is uncharitable and lacking in altruism, except in so far as his economic position may be improved by it.

[1] Spranger (27).

The man with the æsthetic attitude is unambitious. The highest good is to be found in form and harmony. Knowledge is no good for its own sake, but only in relation to other pieces of knowledge which fit together harmoniously. To describe an object in terms of its utility or practical value destroys its beauty. The æsthetic man is not unsocial, but he tends to be eccentric, and since he introduces æsthetic values into his social relationships he is apt to be difficult and intolerant.

The social attitude is guided by living through and for others. It is in sharp contrast with the economic attitude and it also contrasts with the æsthetic attitude. A man with a predominantly æsthetic attitude, for example, avoids people who live in poverty and squalor, whereas the man with a predominantly social attitude feels that the greater the degree of poverty and squalor the more necessary it is to give help, and the more he seeks out such people.

The political attitude is characterised by power. Knowledge is useful only in so far as it leads to the gaining of power over other people. Power may be acquired by tact or by force or by any other available method. A man with the political attitude tends in his social relationships to mix with people so that he may dominate them.

The religious attitude directs the individual towards the highest possible values of an integrated life. An intellectual system as such implies nothing in regard to total value. The religious attitude has a strong positive social relationship, although in certain cases the religious man may try to free himself entirely from the world and live the life of a hermit.

For purposes of description, the types are isolated, but Spranger admits that each attitude may be found in varying degrees in all personalities. In general there is a correspondence between the economic and the political attitudes, between social and religious, and between æsthetic and theoretical. On the other hand, both social and religious attitudes are opposed to the theoretical, and economic and political attitudes are opposed to æsthetic and religious attitudes.

Vernon and Allport[1] devised a situational questionnaire which is intended to give a picture of the relative predominance of these six values in the personality as a whole. It is claimed that the test has high reliability and validity, and that it is useful for such purposes as vocational guidance.

[1] Vernon and Allport (35).

CONCLUSION

Whatever methods are used to measure personality, temperament and types the effect of a culture on fashioning the behaviour of the individuals who compose it should never be overlooked. The cultural influence may be of more far-reaching importance on how an individual's behaviour patterns develop than many innate characteristics with which he may have been endowed. Interest then becomes focused on the cultural *ethos* and *eidos* and their effect on behaviour and development. This is elaborated in the work of such anthropologists as Benedict,[1] Mead [2] and Bateson,[3] and it has been mentioned in many parts of this book.[4]

REFERENCES

1. ALLPORT, G. W., "A Test for Ascendance-Submission ". *J. Abn. Soc. Psychol.*, 1928, 23, 118–36.

2. ——, *Personality: A Psychological Interpretation*. New York: Holt, 1937, pp. 588.

3. ——, and VERNON, P. E., *Studies in Expressive Movement*. New York: Macmillan, 1933, pp. 269.

4. BATESON, G., *Naven*. Cambridge: University Press, 1936, pp. 286.

5. BECK, S. J., *An Introduction to the Rorschach Method*. New York: Amer. Orthopsychiatric Assoc., 1937, pp. 278.

6. BENEDICT, R., *Patterns of Culture*. London: Routledge, 1935, pp. 291.

7. BROWN, S. Clement, "The Methods of Social Case Workers ". Chapter 15 in *The Study of Society* (Ed., F. C. Bartlett and others). London: Kegan Paul, 1939, pp. 498.

8. BURT, C., *The Factors of the Mind*. London: University of London Press, 1940, pp. 509.

9. CATTELL, R. B., *A Guide to Mental Testing*. London: University of London Press, 1936, pp. 312.

10. EARL, C. J. C., "Some Methods of Assessing Temperament and Personality ". Chapter 10 in *The Study of Society* (Ed., F. C. Bartlett and others). London: Kegan Paul, 1939, pp. 498.

11. ESTES, S. J., "Judging Personality from Expressive Behavior ". *J. Abn. Soc. Psychol.*, 1938, 33, 217–36.

12. GARVEY, C. R., "Comparative Body-build of Manic-depressive and Schizophrenic Patients ". *Psychol. Bull.*, 1930, 30, 567–8.

13. HARTSHORNE, H., and MAY, M. A., *Studies in Deceit*, New York: Macmillan, 1928, pp. 306.

14. HARVEY, S. M., "A Preliminary Investigation of the Interview ". *Brit. J. Psychol.*, 1938, 28, 263–87.

15. HEIDBREDER, E., "Measuring Introversion and Extraversion ". *J. Abn. Soc. Psychol.*, 1926, 21, 120–38.

16. JUNG, C. G., *Psychological Types*. London: Kegan Paul, 1924, pp. 654.

17. KENT, G. H., and ROSANOFF, A. J., "A Study of Association in Insanity ". *Amer. J. Insan.*, 1910, 67, 37–96: 317–90.

---

[1] Benedict (6).   [2] Mead (21).   [3] Bateson (4).
[4] It is further elaborated in my book, *The Framework of Human Behaviour*.

18. KRETSCHMER, E., *Physique and Character*. London : Kegan Paul, 1925, pp. 266.

19. MacCURDY, J. T., *War Neuroses*. Cambridge : University Press, 1918, pp. 132.

20. McDOUGALL, W. *National Welfare and National Decay*. London : Methuen, 1921, pp. 214.

21. MEAD, M., *Sex and Temperament in Three Primitive Societies*. London : Routledge, 1935, pp. 335.

22. NEYMANN, C. A., and KOHLSTEDT, K. D., " A New Diagnostic Test for Introversion-Extraversion ". *J. Abn. Soc. Psychol.*, 1929, **23**, 483-4.

23. OLDFIELD, R. C., *The Psychology of the Interview*. London : Methuen, 1941, pp. 144.

24. PRESSEY, S. L., " A Group-scale for Investigating the Emotions ". *J. Abn. Soc. Psychol.*, 1921, **16**, 55-64.

25. RODGER, A., " The Work of the Vocational Adviser ". Chapter XI in *The Study of Society* (*Ed.*, F. C. Bartlett and others). London : Kegan Paul, 1939, pp. 498.

26. RORSCHACH, H., *Psychodiagnostik*. Berne : Huber, 1932, pp. 230.

27. SPRANGER, E., *Types of Men*. Halle : Niemeyer, 1928, pp. 402.

28. SYMONDS, P. M., *Diagnosing Personality and Conduct*. New York : Appleton-Century, 1931, pp. 602.

29. TERMAN, L. M., and MILES, C. C., *Sex and Personality*. New York : McGraw-Hill, 1936, pp. 600.

30. THURSTONE, L. L., " The Measurement of Social Attitudes ". *J. Abn. Soc. Psychol.*, 1931, **26**, 249-69.

31. ——, and THURSTONE, T. G., " A Neurotic Inventory ". *J. Soc. Psychol.*, 1930, **1**, 3-30.

32. VERNON, P. E., " Can the ' Total Personality ' be Studied Objectively ? " *Character and Personality*, 1935, **4**, 1-10.

33. ——, " The Assessment of Psychological Qualities by Verbal Methods ". *Ind. Hlth. Res. Bd. Rep.*, 1938, No. 83, pp. 124.

34. ——, " Questionnaires, Attitude Tests and Rating Scales ". Chapter 9 in *The Study of Society* (*Ed.*, F. C. Bartlett and others). London : Kegan Paul, 1939, pp. 498.

35. ——, and ALLPORT, G., " A Test for Personal Values ". *J. Abn. Soc. Psychol.*, 1931, 26, 231-48.

36. WATSON, G. B., " The Measurement of Fair-Mindedness ". *Teachers' Coll. Contrib. to Educ.*, 1925, No. 176, pp. 97.

37. MUSCIO, B., " The Influence of the Form of a Question ". *Brit. J. Psychol.*, 1918, **8**, 351-89.

CHAPTER VII

MOTIVATION

It has been found convenient to classify the simpler forms of behaviour into different types, each of which possesses certain features which distinguish it from the others. So far as the simpler organisms are concerned this procedure possesses some advantages, but, as we shall see, it is not so certain that the same classification helps in describing the complex types of behaviour which are shown by human beings.

TROPISMS

The simplest form of behaviour is the *tropism*. Some authorities [1] define it as, " any unlearnt form of response not under the control of a nervous system ", illustrating it by such types of behaviour as the tendency of the sunflower to face the sun, of the roots emerging from a seed to go downwards into the ground, and of the shoots to go upwards, so that even if the seed is planted upside down the plant that emerges will right itself. Other authorities [2] think that this definition limits the concept too severely, and they introduce the idea of bilateral similarity. They regard as tropistic any behaviour which leads from asymmetrical to symmetrical stimulation. They regard, therefore, the behaviour of the moth towards the candle flame as of this type. The moth flying past the flame has one side of its body stimulated by the light from the flame more intensively than the other side. The nervous connections lead the moth to turn until both sides of its body are stimulated equally, and in the moth's case it turns towards the candle flame and approaches it until it comes so close that the heat reverses the reaction, and it attempts to turn away again. Similarly, the reaction of a baby's eyes in following a light which is moved from side to side in front of it is regarded as being of the same type.

These authorities classify tropistic responses into those that are positive or negative (i.e. which determine a movement towards or away from a given stimulus), and they name the tropisms according to the kind of stimulus that is given. Thus there are positive and negative geotropic, phototropic, chemo-

[1] See, for example, Hunter (25), p. 50.
[2] See Loeb (31) and Crozier and Hoagland (10).

tropic, heliotropic, etc., responses. On these principles Loeb and Crozier have experimented with the effect of presenting two or more stimuli simultaneously, e.g. by putting young rats on an inclined plane and directing a light towards them. The rats being negatively geotropic (i.e. tending to go upwards rather than downwards) and negatively phototropic, the general path that they will follow can be predicted. They believe that the more complex types of behaviour may often be reducible to combinations of elementary tropistic reactions of this kind. Their work has not been accepted without criticism, however, for it is pointed out that the deductions about the path which will be followed are often based on the *average* responses of the group of organisms on which the experiments are performed, and that individual variations from this average are too often ignored. In these circumstances it is argued that the theory is not of much practical value for purposes of either explaining or predicting the response of any given member of the group. Furthermore, the effects of learning, which may modify the reactions of the individuals to the original stimuli, may become established in the different individuals with different degrees of rapidity, and thus lead to an even greater variability in the behaviour of the members of the group than occurred when the experiment was begun. To consider merely the arithmetical average of the group's behaviour, therefore, becomes more and more meaningless the longer the experiments are continued.

REFLEXES

The next type of behaviour is known as the *reflex*, which has been defined as a uniform response to a simple sensory stimulus. Bilateral similarity does not enter here, for the organism may be in as unsymmetrical a position in regard to the stimulus when its reaction is completed as it was at the beginning. Some authorities have classified reflexes into three groups, (1) those which are involuntary, e.g. the contraction of the iris in the presence of light and its expansion in darkness, (2) those which are partially voluntary, e.g. sneezing and coughing, which may be controlled up to a point but which become involuntary beyond that point, and (3) voluntary, e.g. the inhibition of the reflex withdrawal of the hand on touching something hot, if such inhibition is demanded by the circumstances as, for example, when a valuable plate is taken out of a hot oven.

Other authorities describe reflexes in more purely physio-

logical terms, and discuss the way the stimulation of a sensory end organ effects the transmission of a nerve impulse up the afferent nerve fibre to the spinal cord, and how the impulse proceeds from there down an efferent nerve fibre to the appropriate muscle to cause a reaction. Reduced to its simplest form the description is often presented in terms of a simple reflex arc, as if only one sensory nerve fibre, one spinal nerve cell, and one motor nerve fibre were involved. This in fact is never so. Many nerve fibres are stimulated, and the impulses which reach the spinal cord often cause inhibition as well as excitation. Furthermore, many muscles are brought into operation in the subsequent reaction, some being excited and others inhibited, and the final response is often graded to meet particular situations. The whole reaction is not so mechanical as one might deduce from some of the descriptions, and in some of the reflexes, e.g. the scratch reflex, the response is organised so as to meet the varying conditions of stimulation.

When two or more reflex actions follow one another successively a type of response known as a *chain reflex* is often established. Locomotion and swallowing are offered as examples to illustrate this more complex type of reaction. Here a stimulus *A* gives rise to a response *B* which, when it occurs, acts as a stimulus for response *C*, and so on down the chain. Locomotion is rhythmical and periodic, the chain of responses and stimuli occurring over and over again—thus response *N* acts as a stimulus for response *A*, and the whole sequence begins over again. Swallowing is unidirectional and non-repetitive.

CONDITIONED REFLEXES

Another complication of the simple reflex has been elicited by the work of Pavlov [1] on *conditioned reflexes*. In the typical experiment, which has been often described, Pavlov started from the well-known fact that a dog's mouth will water as a result of the taste of food. This is an example of an unconditioned reflex. It needs no explanation : it is part of the natural behaviour of the dog. The taste of food is the unconditioned stimulus and salivation is the unconditioned response. Pavlov then showed that if a bell is rung a short time before the food is presented, then after this sequence a bell—food—salivation had been repeated a number of times, the bell by itself would cause the salivation. This phenomenon Pavlov called a conditioned reflex.

[1] Pavlov (36).

The bell, which previously was entirely neutral and caused no salivation, has, by association with the food, acquired some of the characteristics of the latter, so that the response which was previously made to the taste of food alone is now made to the sound of the bell. The bell is known as the conditioning stimulus, and this new behavioural pattern as a conditioned reflex. Further researches showed that in favourable circumstances secondary and even tertiary conditioned reflexes could be established.[1] In the secondary conditioned reflex a new stimulus, e.g. a bright light, is presented before the sound of the bell, until eventually the light itself acts as a conditioning stimulus.

A number of remarkable features of conditioned reflexes were then laid bare, and as a result of his work Pavlov was led to the conclusion that the more complex series of actions occurring as a result of habit formation and learning could be reduced to combinations of simple conditioned reflexes. Thus he maintained,[2] " it is obvious that the different kinds of habits based on training, education and discipline of any sort are nothing but a long chain of conditioned reflexes ". Watson [3] has elaborated this view into the doctrines of Behaviorism. Other authorities, however, regard it as more convenient, more instructive, and, in particular, more correct to distinguish other types of learning from conditioned reflexes. The typical conditioned reflex experiment is performed in highly artificial conditions in which slight external stimuli interfere with the creation of a regular response, whereas most ordinary learning takes place in spite of the existence of many external disturbances. Then the response to the conditioning stimulus is not the same as that to the unconditioned stimulus : the dog eats the food with which it is presented, but it only salivates when the bell is sounded. It makes no attempt to eat the bell. The dog must therefore differentiate in some way between the two stimuli, and we may justifiably regard the two responses as qualitatively different. Again Grindley [4] has shown that some simple habits can be established *de novo* and not simply through the association of a new stimulus with one that causes an innate response. The importance of his contribution is that he performed his experiments in conditions which were very similar to those in which the conditioned reflex experiments are performed ; that he started from a situation in which there was no relevant unconditioned behaviour pattern—

[1] Hull (24).   [2] Pavlov (36), p. 393.
[3] Watson (42), (43). [4] Grindley (16).

no innate connection between a particular stimulus and a particular form of response ; and yet he showed that such an association may be built up by a reward acting *retroactively* and establishing a connection between a stimulus and a response which had occurred *before* the reward.

Finally Pavlov's theory implies a fine localisation of conditioned reflexes in the cortex. Pavlov himself says,[1]

> All these conditioned reflexes must have definite representation in the cerebral cortex in one or another definite group of cells. One such group of cells must be connected with one definite activity of the organism, another group with another activity : one group may determine a positive activity while another may inhibit an activity. The cerebral cortex can accordingly be represented as an exceedingly rich mosaic or as an extremely complicated " switch-board ".

Lashley,[2] however, has shown that the capacity to learn depends —at any rate in the rat—on the total amount of cortex an animal possesses rather than on the possession of this, that or the other portion of it, and that the learning and retention of habits are not dependent on finely localised structures.

INSTINCT

The next type of behaviour which calls for some detailed examination is that which goes by the name of *instinct*. An instinct is a definite impulse, common to all the members of the same species, to perform a certain pattern of activity without training. The emphasis in this definition rests on the words " pattern of activity ", and this being so many examples can be given of the way in which an instinct differs from a chain reflex or from a complicated conditioned reflex. It may be pointed out, for instance, that whereas in the chain reflex or the conditioned reflex the same series of stimuli and responses always occur in the same order, in the instinct there may be considerable modification in detail, although the general pattern remains the same. Hobhouse [3] quotes as an example of this a bird which usually builds its nest of rushes finding itself in a district without rushes and substituting horse-hair ; or a bird which usually builds its nest on the ground, taking to the trees if there happen to be cats in the neighbourhood. In both these cases the general pattern of the nest remains the same, it is only the minor details of the behaviour which have been altered. Again the different

[1] Pavlov (36), p. 219.   [2] Lashley (29).   [3] Hobhouse (20), Chap. **6.**

elements forming the pattern of an instinct may be performed in a different order on different occasions. Finally, an instinctive action, e.g. nest-building, may be interrupted for a time while other types of behaviour are engaged upon, and then be taken up again later at the point where it was interrupted. Interrupted chain-reflex actions, however, usually have to be started from the very beginning again and cannot be taken up from the point where they were interrupted. And certainly their sequence of reactions cannot be transposed in the way that occurs in instincts.

Instinctive patterns of behaviour appear most clearly in the behaviour of insects, where they are relatively inflexible and relatively simple, and in the behaviour of birds, where the pattern is more complex and there is greater scope for modification. It is on these types of animal that most of the investigations of instinctive behaviour have been made. There is no doubt that so far as they are concerned the concept of instinct is an extremely useful one for describing a particular kind of behaviour. Illustrations are often given [1] of the rigidity of the behavioural pattern in wasps and bees, and of its plasticity among ants where it often reaches a high level. At the same time the modifiability is distinguishable from that which is due to the application of intelligence by reason of the fact that it is a specific form of plasticity confined to a particular behavioural pattern, and that outside that pattern the behaviour of even the ant *Atta* [2]—which uses leaves to form manure on which a fungus is grown to provide it with its staple food—is extremely circumscribed and rigid. That is to say, the concept of intelligence is introduced to describe the general level of an animal's adaptation to changing circumstances over the whole range of its behaviour. When this adaptation is narrowly restricted to a few particular patterns the concept of instinct is considered to be a more useful description. Furthermore, such modifications as occur are for the most part modifications which all members of the species adopt : in the case of intelligence, however, the adaptations to meet changing circumstances are far more an individual matter. Nevertheless, as writers like Hobhouse have insisted, an exact distinction between the realms of instinct and of intelligence is very difficult to make.

CLASSIFICATION OF INSTINCTS

Finding that the concept of instinct serves a useful purpose in describing certain types of behavioural pattern, many writers

---

[1] See, for example, Hingston (19).   [2] Huxley (26), pp. 37-40.

have attempted to provide a classification of the different forms
instinctive behaviour may take. The basis of classification has
varied, some authorities basing their classification on the stimulus
that gives rise to the reaction, others using the response that is
made, and others using the impulse that arises. The number of
instincts that have emerged in the classifications of different
authorities has also varied widely : some have only two—a
self-preserving instinct and a race-preserving instinct—others
have a large number. In McDougall's [1] classification there were
18 instincts (or *propensities*). These varied in complexity very
considerably, ranging all the way from coughing, breathing and
excretion which are more usually classified under the heading
of reflexes, up to food-seeking and mating. Ginsberg [2] has
classified them into three main groups with various subdivisions
in each group. His classification is :—

ROOT INTERESTS	SPECIFIC FORMS
Supply of bodily needs.	Hunger, Thirst, Excretion, Exercise, Rest, Sleep, etc.
Needs arising out of man's relation to physical world. Mind making itself at home in the world.	Avoidance of injury, investigation. Construction.
Needs arising out of relations to other life. Needs of others.	Response and craving for response, specialized in : Dependence, Protection, The Sex relation.

It will be seen therefore that there is considerable diversity
of opinion among the different authorities as to the best method
of classification.

Now although the concept of instinct is not an *explanatory*
concept, and although it tells us nothing more fundamental about
an animal's behaviour to say it is due to such and such an instinct,
yet so far as the behaviour of insects and birds at any rate is
concerned, the concept does have value in grouping together
types of behaviour which are more closely related to one another
than they are to other types of behaviour. When we come to
the behaviour of human beings, however, it is more doubtful
whether the concept in the way in which it has been defined
serves any very useful purpose. The reason is that the expression

[1] McDougall (33), pp. 97–8.   [2] Ginsberg (14), p. 141.

of man's fundamental impulses is so greatly affected by the customs and traditions, the norms and the pressures of the society into which he is born, that it becomes a matter of extreme difficulty to pick out from the behaviour of the adult man that part which rests on an instinctive basis from that part which is due to the effects of the cultural pattern. Even when the task is successfully accomplished it is questionable whether anything of value is attained thereby. In recent years a large number of psychologists have come to realise the truth of this, and there has been a tendency to regard the concept of instinct as out of date and useless. Some of them, however, believe that the difficulty can be overcome by changing the name of instinct to propensity or drive or appetite or erg, as if a change of name could effect an alteration in the character of the phenomenon—although in some cases, it is true, they not only change the name but use the new name to describe an entirely different type of behaviour from that which is referred to as instinctive when the behaviour of insects or birds is being described. Let us look at this matter a little more closely by considering some of the fundamental activities of mankind which have often been included in any classification of instincts.

THE MATERNAL INSTINCT

Maternal behaviour is often regarded as one of the most fundamental instincts of animals and men. It is, for example, referred to by McDougall [1] as " Nature's brightest and most beautiful invention ", and he believes that, " it was this ' invention ' which alone rendered possible the development of a highly intelligent species such as *Homo Sapiens,* and which also gave to his nature, conduct and institutions all that is truly admirable in the moral sense ".

Warden [2] in fact found by experiment that this " drive " was stronger in rats than were the drives of thirst, hunger and sex, and examples of the so-called maternal instinct are too numerous to need description here. Very likely it is true that this behaviour has an innate basis, yet the effect of the culture on the way in which it expresses itself in mankind is so extremely varied that it is doubtful whether the concept of an instinct helps us to describe the behaviour. It is a far cry from the behaviour of hens with chicks to the very varied forms of response

[1] McDougall (32), pp. 130 and 131.   [2] Warden (41).

that are found among members of the human species. Rivers,[1] for instance, reports that owing to the widespread practice of adoption it is very difficult to get genealogies from the Murray Islanders. Similarly, it is reported that in the Andaman Islands [2] it is a very rare thing to find a child over the age of six years residing with its own parents. To request parents to be allowed to adopt one of their children is considered as a compliment, and the foster-parents treat their adopted children with precisely the same kindness as they treat their own children. Other cultures have adopted different modes of behaviour, e.g. acquiring a child by paying for the services of a midwife, or being the first person to plant the leaf of a tree in front of the house in which a child is born.[3]

Again in Ancient China [4] it was accepted as a principle that there could be only one wife, and therefore only one mother. Consequently the children of the secondary wives were regarded as the children of the principal wife and they paid her, and not their blood mothers, the high respect which was regarded as the due of a mother. On this principle it was not necessary to bring a child into the world in order to have a son : it was sufficient if one was the principal wife and for one of the other wives to have a son. Similarly, too, if the principal wife happened in the course of time to be discarded by her husband, all the children treated her successor as their mother.

In other societies children are used in payment of debts or sold into slavery. In many, infanticide is a common practice. Sometimes it is regarded as proper to have an equal number of boys and girls, and in such cases if there is an excess of one or the other sex they are killed off. Sometimes, in the Solomon Islands,[5] it is regarded as too much trouble to bring up children, so young adults are purchased from other neighbouring groups.

So, whatever the fundamental physiological mechanism may be, it is clear from these examples that the actual forms the behaviour takes are shaped by very strong cultural forces.

Sex

The influence of the cultural environment on differences in sexual behaviour might be illustrated very well by the different customs and mores in the countries of Western civilization where the attitude of men towards women and the social expectation

[1] Rivers (37), vol. 5, p. 126.   [2] Klineberg (28), p. 258.
[3] Ibid., p. 258.   [4] Ibid., p. 259.   [5] Ibid, p. 260.

I

which influences the way they behave towards them varies according to the different cultural patterns which have been built up. A comparative analysis of these differences has not so far been worked out in any detail, but we may turn to Mead's brilliant analysis [1] of three primitive communities to illustrate what we have in mind.

Mead extends the theory developed by Benedict [2]—that a society's cultural pattern is a most important determinant of the behaviour of its adult members—to cover the differences in the way the sexes behave. She describes three tribes. The first, the Arapesh, is a gentle, peace-loving people among whom there is a minimum of distinction between men and women. Boys and girls play the same games which are mild and co-operative and never competitive. The child is brought up as much by the father as by the mother, and its development is lovingly fostered with much petting and fondling. There is no acknowledged temperamental difference between the sexes in adulthood, and a sex relationship is as likely to be initiated by a woman as by a man. Sex is a serious business, and there are few liaisons or casual encounters. Those who are maladjusted in this tribe are the violent, aggressive men and the violent, aggressive women. This offers an immediate contrast to our own society in which it is the unaggressive men and the aggressive women who tend to be the deviants.

The second tribe Mead describes, the Mundugumor, also assume that men and women have similar temperamental endowments. But whereas among the Arapesh they are both regarded as gentle and unaggressively sexed, among the Mundugumor they are both expected to be violent and competitive and aggressively sexed. The children are born into a hostile world. Both the father and the mother resent the birth. They are suckled with great haste, and are returned to their baskets as soon as they stop sucking even for a moment. They therefore hurriedly gulp down what they can while they can, and in the process they frequently choke. This infuriates both them and their mother. The suckling situation is characterised by a contest and a struggle instead of by affection and reassurance such as is found among the Arapesh. Similarly, too, the love-affairs of the young unmarried people are characterised by violence and passion rather than by tenderness or romance. Those who deviate from this pattern are the unaggressive, gentle

[1] Mead (34).   [2] Benedict (7).

men and women. It is the same type for both sexes, as it is in the first tribe, although the type itself is very different.

Finally Mead describes a third tribe, the Tchambuli, who live within 100 miles of each of the other two tribes. Here it is the women who have the real power and who own the property and who do all the important work. The men have to wheedle what they want out of the women by means of languishing looks and soft words. In a group of men there is constant bickering and quarrelling and strain and watchfulness and catty remarks : but the lives of the women are singularly unclouded by personal remarks or by quarrelling. The men sit about in a highly charged atmosphere of courtship, none knowing on whom a woman's choice will fall. It is the women who are supposed to be more highly sexed : the men are much more easily able to wait. In this tribe, therefore, we see a reversal of the social expectation found in our own society. The more virile, aggressive and actively sexed males, and the gentle, maternal females tend to be the deviants.

Apart from these differences in sexual behavioural patterns as a result of cultural influences, there are a few other differences to which we may draw attention. A Kaffir, for example, despises a wife who is taken for love, i.e. with no bride price, with no less fervour than people in our own society, with its ideals directed towards romantic love, despise a man who makes a loveless but lucrative marriage. The manifestations of jealousy too seem to be largely culturally conditioned : sometimes a wife's children by another man are accepted by a husband as his own, and sometimes a woman will beg her husband to take another wife so as to relieve her of some part of her domestic duties. The custom of wife lending as a mark of respect for a guest has also been regarded by some authorities as being evidence of the absence of any fundamental feeling of exclusive possession of a wife. It may be, however, that the feeling of exclusive possessiveness exists as strongly in those communities as in our own : that jealousy is only non-existent when the husband is in the position of offering his wife, and that he would be as much affronted if she slept with another man without his permission as most husbands in our own community would be. It may be that the attitude he adopts towards, and the satisfaction he obtains from, offering his wife to his guest is comparable with that which the English gentleman experiences when he produces a bottle of vintage port or of Napoleon brandy for his.

PUGNACITY

McDougall and other authorities have listed aggressiveness or pugnacity among the instincts. Several regard assertiveness as co-extensive with aggressiveness ; others, e.g. McDougall,[1] regard them as separate instincts. In McDougall's view combative behaviour will be evoked by the thwarting or obstruction of any animal in its pursuit of a goal, and he points out that some species are equipped with special organs of combat. He regards assertiveness and submissiveness as a reflection of the acceptance of a particular status within a social group. He confines assertiveness and submissiveness to the species which are gregarious, though pugnacity is not so limited.

The view that aggressiveness is a fundamental tendency in human beings is also to be found in much of the psychoanalytic literature. For instance, Adler's [2] view is that everybody possesses an impulse to dominate through compensating for a real or imagined inferiority. The feeling arises in childhood when the child naturally feels weak in relation to the outside world. His actions are determined for him by his parents who often make him do many things he would rather not do, and prevent him from doing others which he wants to do. The same feeling persists after the child has grown up. Then, too, he feels insignificant and impotent in the face of society with its traditions and conventions. Some children and adults feel this sense of inferiority more strongly than others : it is particularly likely to be strong in someone who suffers from a physical handicap, such as low stature, a club foot, a cleft palate and so on. And the more strongly this sense of inferiority is felt the stronger will be the attempt to compensate for it by trying to demonstrate superiority in some other way, and by setting an ambitious goal to achieve. So long as the individual possesses the necessary ability he will manage to achieve his goal, but many people are not so lucky : in spite of their acute inferiority feelings they do not have the ability to achieve the high goals they set themselves as a result of this feeling. These become neurotic.

Apart from physical infirmities there are various other factors which determine the inferiority feeling and its resulting compensations. One is the ordinal position of the individual in his family. Adler maintains (without much evidence to support the view, it is true) that younger or youngest children are more likely to achieve eminence than older children, for older children

[1] McDougall (32).   [2] Adler (1).

have at least the younger children over whom they can feel superior : the younger children have no one below them. The younger children will therefore tend to set their goals higher than the older children in compensation, and consequently, if they possess the necessary ability, they will be more likely to achieve eminence. It should also follow from this theory that a larger number of younger than of older children would be found among the neurotics, but there is no evidence to support this.

At all events this brief summary of some of Adler's views shows that whether it is strong or weak everyone will possess some tendency towards aggressiveness as a compensation for their real or imagined inferiority to other people or to the world at large. The impulse could presumably be diminished if children were less repressed by their parents and teachers, but some degree of thwarting would still persist through the influence of social factors.[1]

In the Freudian theory there seem to be several lines of argument which lead to the conclusion that aggressiveness and even warfare are inevitable. In the first place aggressiveness may be traced to the pleasure a child gets in sucking at the mother's breast. During the process he is likely at some time or other to bite the breast. Then the biting will become associated with the pleasure he obtains from the food (presumably much in the manner of the establishment of a conditioned reflex), and later on a similar type of satisfaction will be obtained from crushing, mutilating and grinding. Some Analysts [2] have even gone so far as to point out that animals which pursue prey kill it by means of tooth and claw. The analogy in this case does not bear a very deep analysis, however, when it is remembered that there are birds like the hawk which kill their prey by means of beak and claw, and that these, having been in their youth hatched from eggs, have not had the advantage and consequent pleasure which mammals enjoy of biting their mothers' nipples.

A second line of argument traces aggressiveness to the Œdipus complex and to the concept of ambivalence—e.g. liking and disliking a person or object at one and the same time. The child, being in more intimate contact from the earliest days of its life with its mother than with its father, will tend to develop a strong emotional attachment to her. As a result of this he (the case is

---

[1] See, for example, Durbin and Bowlby (11). See also Harding (17) for an excellent analysis of aggressiveness from many points of view.
[2] Hopkins (22), p. 98.

somewhat more complicated with a girl who has to become more strongly emotionally attached to her father than to her mother) develops a high degree of jealousy of his father, resenting his father's claims on his mother. He also adopts an attitude of resentment towards his parents, owing to the fact that they control his actions and thwart or frustrate him from doing everything he wants to. Combined with this resentment, however, is the gratitude he feels towards his parents for their satisfaction of his needs, and the pressure of social conventions which force him to show affection towards his father. This vast conflict between the pressure to like and the pressure to dislike is resolved in most cases by a repression of the dislike into the unconscious mind. Yet although repressed this antagonism is not destroyed : it continues to exist in the unconscious with its energy undisposed until an appropriate object appears on which it may vent its fury. Such an object is a socially approved bogy like the Jews or the Jesuits or a common enemy. In such cases we can join with those around us and with full social approval transfer our repressed hatred of our father on to the common enemy.

Some authorities believe that this offers a very satisfactory explanation for the phenomenon of war. One comes, it is said, to identify one's native land with one's mother, for one's native land feeds and clothes and educates us. We refer to her as our " mother land " (though the fact that in many countries individuals show " patriotism " towards their " fatherland " rather than " matriotism " towards their " motherland " is quietly ignored), and we come to love her truly as we love our flesh-and-blood mother. " When foreign troops threaten our country, we describe their action as one of invading or assaulting her, thus showing who in our unconscious minds we think they are. All the allies in the Great War, for example, felt *outraged* by the *rape* of Belgium." [1] " Unconscious fear of an assault on our mother, therefore, is largely responsible for the clamour that our country shall be ' protected ' against potential evil father-figures by the largest army or navy or air-fleet which we can wring out of the taxpayers." [2]

Finally, the symbolical significance of many weapons of war is often called in evidence. Modern weapons of war are not only pointed and long, but they also project particles into the interior of bodies. Their genital significance is believed to be betrayed by this fact. Furthermore, it is argued that the object

[1] Hopkins (22), p. 131.   [2] Ibid., p. 131.

in war is to mutilate the enemy so as to reduce his *potency* (i.e. symbolically to castrate him). In peace-time the object of aggressiveness is to mutilate one's business rivals, or, if one is a small boy, to mutilate flies—presumably also with the same unconscious intention as is supposed to exist in time of war.

Although the Analytic view gives what purports to be an explanation of aggressiveness and of war, and although it appears to possess such a high degree of plausibility (particularly perhaps through its choice of words) as to appear to some people in the light of a glaringly obvious truth, a brilliant piece of inductive analysis, or a fundamental principle of human behaviour accepted with almost religious fervour, yet it remains a fact that it has never been experimentally proved, and it appears to other people to be so basically absurd, particularly in its modern refinements, as almost to be silly. Like most of the Analytic doctrines it cannot be disproved : but neither can it be proved.

When we search the anthropological evidence we find that aggressive behaviour, like maternal behaviour or sex behaviour, is largely the result of cultural influences. Benedict [1] describes some of the different attitudes which different groups have adopted towards warfare. Thus the Aztecs used it simply as a means of getting captives for religious sacrifices : they did not fight to kill. In other groups all idea of warfare is understandable : Western methods of warfare are to them on much the same level as a disorderly house brawl is to us. Others cannot understand periods of peace alternating with periods of war, for a period of peace seems to imply that the enemy can be treated as a human being, an idea they do not share. One of the tribes she describes, the Pueblo Indians, are a peace-loving and unaggressive people. They have no tolerance of violence in any form, no indulgence in the exercise of authority, and no delight in any situation in which the individual stands alone and separate from or above the group. And it is reported [2] that the Eskimos could not be made to understand the meaning of battles, and that one of them proposed to send medicine men as missionaries to Western civilisation in order to convert them to the advantages of peace.[3]

---

[1] Benedict (7), pp. 30–2.   [2] Klineberg (28), p. 264.

[3] It is unjustifiable to argue with Steinmetz that these peoples have remained in their primitive condition just because they could not or would not fight and that war is essential to civilisation, for there are other tribes, with a different cultural pattern, who make full use of such opportunities as they may get for warfare, but who have remained in just as primitive a condition as those who have chosen a more peaceful way of life.

Similarly, too, different communities have employed different methods in solving the quarrels between individual members of the community. Sometimes the disputes are carried on with great volubility but with no physical aggression : sometimes they are settled by an appeal to an oracle : sometimes a duel is arranged in which the contestants appear in public and make abusive remarks or sing satirical songs in order to humble the other. The victor is the one who is acclaimed by the audience as the most successful. Afterwards the contestants are on the best of terms with each other. Sometimes the contestants go to a rock or to a large tree armed with sticks and beat the stone or the tree until one of them breaks his stick. This one is then claimed as the victor.

Here again we see therefore the very large number of ways in which society may determine that disputes are to be settled. Our own cultural pattern, which leads us to regard aggressiveness as a fundamental and innate characteristic of human beings, can be matched by many others which make it appear to be an irrelevant superfluity, or even as a highly deviant form of behaviour. Once again it may be repeated that even if it is convenient to regard aggressiveness or maternal behaviour as an instinct when one is discussing the behaviour of some of the lower animals, yet the forces of social pressure and of the cultural pattern modify its mode of expression to such an extent in human beings that it loses its value as a descriptive category.

ACQUISITIVENESS

Many authorities include acquisitiveness as one of the fundamental instincts, and they draw much of their evidence from the behaviour of animals. It has often been pointed out that birds acquire territory at certain seasons of the year, or make collections of straw and feathers and hair and moss : that dogs bury bones and squirrels hoard nuts. Burt [1] has even pointed out that many animals have an acquisitive organ, e.g. the forepaw of the squirrel and the claw of the eagle, and that man and the tribe of apes and monkeys are unique in possessing a hand which is an acquisitive instrument *par excellence*. Yet the view has not passed unchallenged, even so far as animals are concerned. Ginsberg,[2] for example, and Beaglehole [3] have pointed out that things collected for nests, including straw, feathers, etc., as well as territory should be regarded as part of sexual behaviour, and

[1] Burt (9), p. 447.   [2] Ginsberg (15).   [3] Beaglehole (6).

that there is no advantage in considering such acquisitive behaviour as an instinct on its own. Similarly, animals which store food do so as a part of the food-getting impulse, and it is unnecessary and redundant to introduce the concept of an acquisitive instinct to describe it.

In the case of acquisitiveness, therefore, the usefulness of the concept has been questioned, even in connection with the behaviour of animals. It is consequently unlikely that the concept will prove any more useful as a description of a certain type of behaviour in mankind. So far as our own community is concerned the principal evidence is drawn from the behaviour of children and the behaviour of a few highly abnormal adults. Burt,[1] for example, uses his finding that stealing accounts for 80 per cent. of all boyish transgressions as evidence in favour of an acquisitive instinct. By doing so, as he himself points out, he does not concede their true weight to other possible explanations of the behaviour, e.g. hunger, desire to get money for the cinema, spirit of adventure and so on. But when, in addition, he states that in only 16 out of every thousand cases could the delinquency be attributed to sheer inborn acquisitiveness one wonders that he has troubled to introduce the topic of an instinct of acquisition at all, unless he is using the term instinct in a way which is very different from that of other people. Sixteen in every thousand cases is a very different thing from behaviour which is common to all members of the same species. One might, in fact, be led to precisely the opposite conclusion from his illustration. If only 16 in every thousand cases show sheer inborn acquisitiveness, then clearly they diverge very sharply from the norm, in whom it would appear from this evidence that no acquisitive instinct exists.

Many people have pointed out that few children pass through their teens without making collections of stamps, marbles, cigarette cards, shells, eggs or other things. Recent investigations have shown, however, that within the past forty years or so there has been a remarkable change in the collecting habits of children. In 1891 Burk [2] found that over 90 per cent. of children between the ages of 7 and 16 were making collections of one kind or another. In 1927, however, Lehman and Whitty [3] found that only 10 per cent. of children of the same ages were doing so. Beaglehole [4] suggests that the explanation for the change is to

[1] Burt (9), p. 449.   [2] Burk (8).
[3] Lehman and Whitty (30).   [4] Beaglehole (6), p. 259.

be found in the fact that by 1927 there were so many other attractions available for the children, e.g. the cinema, the wireless, dancing, the theatre and so on, that an entirely new set of attitudes and interests had arisen, and the practice of collecting had for the most part receded into the background.

So far as adults are concerned most of the evidence is drawn from a few people—misers, kleptomaniacs and mental-hospital patients. Some mental-hospital patients will spend all their time picking up pins from the floor and hoarding them. Most misers hoard money, but James [1] mentions the case of a miser who hoarded old newspapers. When he died these were found to fill all the rooms of his good-sized house from floor to ceiling, leaving only a few narrow channels between them to give him his living space. Another case, a kleptomaniac, is also reported by James : this man stole his own silver spoons from his own dining-room, and his own pots and pans from his kitchen and stored them in his barn. Subsequently he bought substitutes for them with his own money. But here again to argue that the mode of behaviour of a few highly abnormal individuals can be used to indicate the existence of an acquisitive instinct when the normal pattern is *not* to behave in that particular way is hardly convincing.

So far as primitive communities are concerned many different things are reported by anthropologists to be collected. Thus the Malay collects beads, the North American Indian scalps, the Andaman Islander netting, and the inhabitants of Malekula pigs. Yet this behaviour is not so much evidence in favour of the existence of an acquisitive instinct as a reflection of the type of cultural pattern of the society. Harrisson,[2] for example, reports that the inhabitant of Malekula collects pigs in order to increase his social prestige. Every time he collects another hundred pigs he goes up one rung in the social ladder, until finally when he has collected enough he is symbolically off the top of the ladder, is given the title of " hawk " and may, if he likes, walk about flapping his hands as if in flight. Here the gaining of social prestige is the fundamental motivating force. The fact that in the process many hundreds of pigs have to be collected is incidental to this.

Again in a group of islands to the east of Papua objects of no intrinsic value are sought and then at once circulated in exchange for others.[3] One currency (arm shells) circulates

[1] James (27), Vol. 2, pp. 422–26.   [2] Harrisson (18).   [3] Suttie (40).

clockwise and the other currency (shell necklaces) circulates counter-clockwise among this group of islands. No one gains anything tangible by it. The successful person is he who has passed a greater volume of currency through his hands to the supposed detriment of his competitors. Again it is more reasonable to interpret the behaviour in terms of the particular values which happen to be attached to certain objects by a particular group of people than to explain it in terms of an acquisitive instinct—particularly as every individual gets rid of the objects he collects as soon as he possibly can, and increases his prestige by doing so.

Some primitive communities, in fact, seem to have the opposite of an acquisitive instinct. Benedict [1] describes orgies of destruction among the Kwakiutl Indians. Everyone tries to outdistance everyone else in his distribution of property. If an individual receives a gift and is not able to repay at least double the amount when the time comes for repayment, then he is shamed and loses enormously in prestige. The two ways by which he can show himself to be superior to a rival are to present him with more property than he can return or to destroy a large quantity of his own goods.

> The destruction of goods took many forms. Great potlatch feasts in which quantities of candlefish oil were consumed were reckoned as contests of demolition. The oil was fed lavishly to the guests, and it was also poured upon the fire. Since the guests sat near the fire, the heat of the burning oil caused them intense discomfort, and this also was reckoned as a part of the contest. In order to save themselves from shame, they had to lie unmoved in their places, though the fire blazed up and caught the rafters of the house. The host also must exhibit the most complete indifference to the threatened destruction of his house. Some of the greatest chiefs had a carved figure of a man upon the roof. It was called the vomiter, and a trough was so arranged that a steady stream of the valuable candlefish oil poured out of the figure's open mouth into the house fire below. If the oil feast surpassed anything the guest chief had ever given, he must leave the house and begin preparations for a return feast that would outstrip the one given by his rival. If he believed that it had not equalled a feast that he had previously given, he heaped insults upon his host, who then took some further way of establishing his greatness.[2]

Can one assume the existence of an acquisitive instinct to explain this behaviour? It would be just as reasonable to assume the existence of an instinct of destructiveness.

[1] Benedict (7).   [2] Ibid., pp. 193-4.

Concluding Remarks on Instincts

It should be emphasised once more that I am not trying to maintain that man has no innate behaviour mechanisms of the type which is usually referred to as instinctive. I am not saying that man has no instincts. What I am saying is that it is not so profitable to investigate man's behaviour by analysing and classifying his instincts as it is to consider his behaviour in the light of an interplay between his innate characteristics and the social influences which impinge upon those characteristics. And, further, that the effect of the cultural pattern is in most cases of more importance than a person's innate characteristics. Most people will be moulded by the pattern in which they grow up so as to conform to a considerable degree to that pattern in adulthood. This will hold true with two limitations. The first is that there may be a sudden abandonment of the cultural pattern in very exceptional circumstances, e.g. when the living conditions are made so unfavourable for so many members of the group that they organise a revolution against the established ideas and practices, or—somewhat similarly—after a serious defeat in war. In these conditions there will be an interim period during which there is no predominating cultural pattern until the leading individuals within the community have developed new sentiment habits, attitude habits and interest habits which they will then impose (not always with a very clear consciousness that they are doing so) on the rest of the community and on the rising generation.

The second limitation is that there will always be some individuals within a community whose innate characteristics so far diverge from those of the cultural pattern that instead of being moulded by that pattern and developing according to type they react against the pattern—they may even be driven further away from the pattern because of this—and they become the deviants and the maladjusted individuals within that community. As Benedict has shown, an individual who is a deviant in one community may be the normal, or even the leader, in another community with a different pattern of culture.

Finally, I am not arguing that the cultural pattern inevitably forces everybody to behave in identically the same way. Such an argument would be absurd. Many cultural patterns encourage individuality. But the individuality that is encouraged is of a type that will conform to the existing pattern : that is to say,

variety will exist, but it will be a variety within the limits of a particular configuration of outlook, feeling and behaviour.

SENTIMENTS

If the concept of instinct does not prove very helpful in the description of human motivation, where shall we turn to describe it better ? Perhaps the notions of *sentiments, interests* and *attitudes* are more useful, for one can often see in them the way in which cultural factors are influencing their growth and development, and the way in which they become modified either by some crisis in the individual's own life, e.g. as a result of conversion, great grief, economic distress, falling in love or thwarted ambition ; or by a social crisis of the kind that was mentioned in the last section ; or by social conversion of the type seen frequently during the course of the present war in the sudden changes of sentiments and attitudes of one social group towards another which has unexpectedly become its ally or which has unexpectedly changed from fighting on the same side to fighting on the other ; or by a more gradual change in social customs and ideas, e.g. in the changing social attitude towards, let us say, divorce or criminals or socialism.

A sentiment has been defined as an organised system of emotional dispositions clustered about a particular object or person with the effect that an appropriate emotion tends to be evoked as the occasion requires.[1] Thus if a sentiment of hatred is directed towards a particular person one tends to feel the appropriate emotion as the occasion requires, e.g. pleasure when he is worsted or anger when he is successful.   Many of the text-books on psychology [2] give descriptions of the principal senti-ments that are found in our community, e.g. love, hatred, respect, patriotism, contempt and so on.

Banister [3] has put forward the view that the basis of senti-ments is something innate. He uses the concept in order to explain the herding together of some animals (including man), and as an alternative to the concept of a gregarious instinct. He maintains that herd animals, like the dog, or man, possess " the capacity for the organisation of (their) innate tendencies

---

[1] The sentiment is sometimes distinguished from the *complex* on the ground that the latter contains repressed or morbid elements.   The distinction is on the whole a useful one, but it cannot be adhered to too rigidly, for probably most sentiments contain some repressed elements.   Perhaps the distinction would be better expressed in terms of the relative predominance of the normal or of the morbid elements.

[2] See, for example, McDougall (32), Chap. 17.   [3] Banister (5).

round animate objects " whereas in other animals, like the cat, this capacity is very small. Those animals that possess the tendency, therefore, tend to live in herds while those that do not have it tend to be solitary. One objection to the theory would appear to be that an animal with an innate capacity for organising its tendencies round *inanimate* objects, that is to say with a sentiment-forming tendency of a special type, would be a solitary animal, not a social one. But presumably if the sentiment-forming tendency is found at all it will be found to include animate as well as inanimate objects.

It must be remembered too that the development of sentiments is not *explained* by the supposition that man has a sentiment-forming tendency any more than sex behaviour is " explained " by the assumption that man has a sex instinct. Shand [1] and McDougall [2] and other psychologists who have discussed sentiments have found it more convenient to treat them as types of behaviour (like habit or attitude or interest) which are built up as a result of the individual's experiences. The concept has been exhaustively treated in Shand's monumental work, and more popular extensions have been provided by McDougall. McDougall gives a description of a number of sentiments, among them the sentiment of self-regard. Although McDougall believes that man possesses a specific herd instinct (or gregarious propensity) he thinks that in addition the extension of his sentiment of self-regard binds him to the group to which he belongs in a peculiarly intimate manner. Self-respect, pride, ambition and vanity are forms of the sentiment of self-regard in McDougall's view, but it readily extends itself to include the man's clothes, his house, his books, his wife and children, his school, his profession, his country, and so on, so that he will tend to behave in a similar way when they are the object of praise or blame as he will if he himself is the object.

Hence the paradox, the most important of all truths for social psychology, that these egoistic tendencies of a man's self-regard impel him to strive for the welfare of the group to which he belongs ; they find satisfaction in its prosperity and are painfully thwarted by its failures and shortcomings. And here again a man's sentiment for his group may be, and not uncommonly is, of the same double nature as his sentiment for his child ; that is to say, it is both an extension of his self-regard and a love ; he is not only proud of being an Englishman or an American, but also he regards

---

[1] Shand (38).   [2] McDougall (32), (33).

his nation with affection, admiration, gratitude, holds it to be a thing of value, deserving of his self-sacrificing effort.[1]

McDougall has not, however, sufficiently brought out the implications of his theory. It would seem to follow that in a community which did not foster a possessive attitude in its members the strength of community spirit would be diminished. McDougall himself regards acquisitiveness as something innate, but we have already called this in question. He has not considered the effect on its members of differences in the fundamental social attitudes of different communities. It is more likely that the sentiments that will prove to be of more importance in any community, and which will in consequence affect the way in which most members of that community will behave, will be those—whether acquisitive, communistic, radical or reactionary —which the particular cultural pattern happens to stress most strongly. It may well be that in our own group community spirit or nationalistic sentiment is encouraged by the prevailing social tendencies of acquisitiveness, but if so it should also be remarked that less parochial sentiments may develop in the members of groups who are less strongly directed along these lines : for, as the result of familial and educational influences, most individuals will adopt as they develop the modes of reaction which the community in which they are reared considers to be appropriate.

The prevailing sentiments in the members of any community, therefore, should not be approached as if they were inevitable. Rather they should be considered as a reflection of the influence of the prevailing tendencies in a community on the members of which that community is composed. A complete analysis along these lines still needs to be made.

ATTITUDES AND INTERESTS

Some authorities [2] regard attitudes as a relative transitory type of interest : others regard interests as a transitory type of attitude. For this reason we will consider them both together. It probably depends on the attitude or on the interest which of them should be regarded as the more enduring. It is certainly true that one can have an attitude on a question in which one is not interested, but one cannot have an interest in something without at the same time having an attitude towards it.

Just as no comparative analysis has been made of the different

[1] McDougall (33), p. 236.   [2] Allport (3).

sentiments which tend to be developed in different communities, so also no analysis has been made of the different attitudes and interests which tend to prevail in primitive communities compared with countries in Western civilisation, or even of those in the different countries of Western civilisation which possess fundamentally different social patterns of outlook and behaviour. We shall therefore confine ourselves for the most part to a few remarks about the attitudes and interests which the motivation of our own group is apt to arouse.

We will first of all consider some of the more enduring types of attitude and interest. The fact that our economy is a mixture of wealth, prestige and social class has produced a number of interesting consequences. We obtain money from work and we can purchase other satisfactions with the money we receive. But the relative strengths of these satisfactions with their concomitant attitudes and interests have not been fully explored. Certain things stand out, however. One is the *level of aspiration*.[1] It is true that the height of the aspiration level varies in different people, but it appears that more or less the same degree of aspiration occurs in the different attitudes of any one person, and whatever level an individual may set himself will have an important effect on his social relationships. The aspiration level shows itself, for example, in the extent to which one will compete with others. The strongest degree of competition will be against those who are of approximately the same level as oneself. As Allport[2] points out, one usually sets oneself a goal not so far above one's abilities that one will suffer embarrassment and humiliation if one fails, nor so far below them that one will feel ineffectual and cheap on accomplishing one's task.

The level of aspiration is seen not only in one's work but in one's social behaviour as well. It often goes by the name of " keeping up with the Joneses ". The important thing may be, for example, to buy a car that is slightly better than that of the person who is in the same kind of job as oneself or who lives next door, not to buy one that is better than that of a multi-millionaire. Again, the Wimbledon tennis-player may spend a worried and despondent night over shots that would fill the average player with delight and excitement. In these attitudes we see the effect of a combination of the monetary, social and prestige forces.

When once these interests and attitudes are aroused they

---

[1] See the experimental work of Hoppe (23) and Frank (12).
[2] Allport (3).

tend to persist. One reason for this, as Allport [1] points out, is that they, like other habits, save both time and mental effort, and therefore unless the individual encounters some serious crisis—usually of an emotional kind—which involves the readjustment of many of his ideas and actions he will not bother to change them. Another reason is also developed by Allport [2] in what he calls *functional autonomy*, that is to say, the tendency of an attitude or an interest to persist even after it no longer serves its original purpose. He gives numerous illustrations of this from which we may select the following.

> The miser perhaps learnt his habits of thrift in dire necessity or perhaps his thrift was a symptom of sexual perversion (as Freud would claim) and yet the miserliness persists and even becomes stronger with the years even after the necessity or the roots of the neurosis have been relieved.

Workmanship is another example.

> A good workman feels compelled to do clean-cut jobs even though his security or the praise of others no longer depend upon high standards. In fact in a day of jerrybuilding his workmanlike standards may be to his economic disadvantage. Even so he cannot do a slipshod job. . . . What was once an instrumental technique becomes a master motive.

Finally we will choose one more example.

> The pursuit of literature, the development of good taste in clothes, the use of cosmetics, the acquiring of an automobile, strolls in the public park or a winter in Miami may first serve, let us say, the interests of sex. But every one of these instrumental activities may become an interest in itself, held for a lifetime, long after the erotic motive has been laid away in lavender.

Not all interests and attitudes have this degree of permanence. Some of them as we all know change with age. Strong [3] found, for example, as one might expect, that the desire to be a film actor or airman or cowboy usually became rather less intense at the end of adolescence : on the other hand, some of the interests increased in desirability with age, e.g. the desire to spend nights away from home (in the United States), and the desire to contribute to charities. Still others, e.g. the desire to become an undertaker, were regarded as just as unpleasant at the age of 55 as they were at the age of 35.

---

[1] Allport (3).   [2] Idem. (4), pp. 196–7.
[3] Strong (39).

K

Other interests and attitudes are still more transitory.[1] These are those which are concerned with current fads and fashions described in that masterpiece of contemporary history by F. L. Allen [2] which recalls echoes of the Big Red Scare, Mah Jong, Yes We Have No Bananas, Rudolph Valentino's funeral, Chicago gang warfare, and hundreds of other passing interests in the United States during the 1920's.

Finally it is well to draw attention to Allport's [3] distinction between *public* and *private* attitudes. He points out that most people reserve for themselves the right to say one thing and to think another : that a person caught off his guard may disclose his innermost attitude, but that the direct frontal attack which many psychological enquiries make provokes him to give merely a conventional answer. For this reason Allport concludes that the task of investigating attitudes is difficult and hazardous.

It is a point which it is very necessary for those making a social survey or other survey of attitudes to have constantly in mind. It does not, however, mean that such surveys are valueless, for as Allport points out there is nothing to prove that the private attitude is any more fundamental or significant than the public attitude. Both may be sincerely held. Furthermore, as Murphy, Murphy and Newcomb [4] show, public attitudes represent in essence a degree of liking or disliking of some social customs. Consequently, the degree to which public attitudes are widely held may be taken as a measure of the stability of certain social relationships. This is, however, not true in every case, for the uniformity of attitude may be of a transitory nature due to a certain combination of temporary circumstances (e.g. the great uniformity of attitude towards Mr. Chamberlain at the time of Munich), and there may be as great a uniformity in the opposite direction at a later date. In some cases, therefore, homogeneity of attitude gives no indication of stability of opinion, feeling or action. Nevertheless the suggestion is worth following up. It points in the direction towards which one way of investigating the stability of public attitudes and the stability of social customs might start, and that would be one of the routes too through which one could obtain a measurement of the cultural

---

[1] Some interests and attitudes are more liable to be influenced by propaganda influences than others are. But this question is too wide to be discussed here. It will be discussed with other problems concerned with propaganda in a forthcoming book.

[2] Allen (2).   [3] Allport (3).

[4] Murphy, Murphy and Newcomb (35), p. 1024.

pattern of different communities and of the features of those cultural patterns that would be likely to have most formative influence on the attitudes, feelings, beliefs and actions of the rising generation.

REFERENCES

1. ADLER, A., *The Practice and Theory of Individual Psychology*. London : Kegan Paul, 1932, pp. 352.
2. ALLEN, F. L., *Only Yesterday*. London : Pelican Books, 1938, 2 vols.
3. ALLPORT, G. W., " Attitudes ". Chapter 18 in *A Handbook of Social Psychology*. (*Ed.*, C. Murchison). Worcester, Mass. : Clark University Press, 1935, pp. 1195.
4. ——, *Personality : A Psychological Interpretation*. New York : Holt, 1937, pp. 588.
5. BANISTER, H., " Sentiment and Social Organisation ". *Brit. J. Psychol.* 1932, **22**, 242–9.
6. BEAGLEHOLE, E., *Property*. London : Allen & Unwin, 1931, pp. 326.
7. BENEDICT, R., *Patterns of Culture*. London : Routledge, 1935, pp. 291.
8. BURK, C. F., " The Collecting Instinct ", *Ped. Sem.*, 1900, 7.
9. BURT, C., *The Young Delinquent*. London : University of London Press, 1925, pp. 643.
10. CROZIER, W. J., and HOAGLAND, H. " The Study of Living Organisms ". Chapter 1 in *Handbook of General Experimental Psychology (Ed.*, C. Murchison). Worcester, Mass. : Clark University Press, 1934, pp. 1103.
11. DURBIN, E. F. M., and BOWLBY, J., *Personal Aggressiveness and War*. London : Kegan Paul, 1939, pp. 154.
12. FRANK, J. D., " The Influence of the Level of Performance in One Task on the Level of Aspiration in Another ". *J. Exper. Psychol.*, 1935, **18**, 159–71.
13. GINSBERG, M., *The Psychology of Society*. London : Methuen, 1921, pp. 174.
14. ——, *Studies in Sociology*. London : Methuen, 1932, pp. 211.
15. ——, *Symposium on Property and Possessiveness*. *Brit. J. Psychol. (Med. Sect.*), 1935, **15**, 63–8.
16. GRINDLEY, G. C., " The Formation of a Simple Habit in Guinea-pigs ". *Brit. J. Psychol.*, 1932, **23**, 127–47.
17. HARDING, D. W., *The Impulse to Dominate*. London : Allen & Unwin, 1941, pp. 256.
18. HARRISSON, TOM, " Notes on Class Consciousness and Class Unconsciousness ". *Sociological Review*, 1942, **34**, 147–64.
19. HINGSTON, R. W. G., *Problems of Instinct and Intelligence*. London : Arnold, 1928, pp. 296.
20. HOBHOUSE, L. T., *Mind in Evolution*. London : Macmillan, 1926, revised edn., pp. 483.
21. ——, WHEELER, G. C., and GINSBERG, M., *The Material Culture and Social Institutions of the Simpler Peoples*. London : Chapman & Hall, 1915, pp. 299.
22. HOPKINS, P., *The Psychology of Social Movements*. London : Allen & Unwin, 1938, pp. 284.
23. HOPPE, F., " Erfolg und Misserfolg ". *Psychol. Forsch.*, 1930, **14**, 1–62.
24. HULL, C. L., " The Factor of the Conditioned Reflex ". Chapter 9 in *Handbook of General Experimental Psychology (Ed.*, C. Murchison). Worcester, Mass. : Clark University Press, 1934, pp. 1103.

25. HUNTER, W. S., *Human Behavior.* Chicago : University of Chicago Press, 1928, pp. 355.

26. HUXLEY, J., *Ants.* London : Benn, 1930, pp. 79.

27. James, W., *Principles of Psychology.* London : Macmillan, 1901, 2 vols.

28. KLINEBERG, O., *Race Differences.* New York : Harper, 1935, pp. 366.

29. LASHLEY, K. S., *Brain Mechanisms and Intelligence.* Chicago : University of Chicago Press, 1929, pp. 213.

30. LEHMAN, H. C., and WHITTY, P. A., " The Present Status of the Tendency to Hoard ". *Psychol. Rev.*, 1927, **34**, 48–56.

31. LOEB, J., *Tropisms, Forced Movements and Animal Conduct.* Philadelphia, Pa. : Lippincott, 1918, pp. 209.

32. McDOUGALL, W., *An Outline of Psychology.* London : Methuen, 4th edn. revised, 1928, pp. 456.

33. ——, *The Energies of Men.* New York : Scribners, 1933, pp. 395.

34. MEAD, M., *Sex and Temperament in Three Primitive Societies.* London : Routledge, 1935. pp. 335.

35. MURPHY, G., MURPHY, L. B., and NEWCOMB, T. M., *Experimental Social Psychology.* New York : Harpers, 1937 (revised edn.), pp. 1121.

36. PAVLOV, I. P., *Conditioned Reflexes.* London : Oxford University Press, 1927, pp. 430.

37. RIVERS, W. H. R., *Reports of the Cambridge Anthropological Expedition to Torres Straits (Ed.,* A. C. Haddon). Cambridge : University Press, 1901, Vol. 5.

38. SHAND, A. F., *The Foundations of Character.* London : Macmillan, 1920 (2nd edn.), pp. 578.

39. STRONG, E. K., *Change of Interests with Age.* Stanford University Press, 1931, pp. 235.

40. SUTTIE, I. D., *Symposium on Property and Possessiveness. Brit. J. Psychol. (Med. Sect.)*, 1935, **15**, 51–62.

41. WARDEN, C. J., *Animal Motivation.* New York : Columbia University Press, 1931, pp. 502.

42. WATSON, J. B., *Behavior : An Introduction to Comparative Psychology.* New York : Holt, 1914, pp. 439.

43. ——, *Behaviorism,* London : Kegan Paul, 1931, pp. 308.

CHAPTER VIII

MENTAL MECHANISMS AND EMOTION

INTRODUCTORY

The organisation which keeps a human being in adjustment with his fellows and with his environment is very complicated : it is a reflection of the combination of his innate capacities and the physical and social influences that he has encountered in the particular social group in which he happens to have been brought up. The relative strength of the reaction of different individuals to the same situation consequently varies, and it is this individuality which enables some people to remain unscathed by experiences that would induce an acute form of maladjustment in others. Again, among those who become maladjusted some may react in one way and others in quite a different way. Nevertheless, in spite of this diversity, it is possible to describe not more than a few main types of maladjustment which those individuals who become maladjusted in our society exhibit. Many of these are in fact of such common occurrence in their milder forms that they can hardly be regarded as maladjustments at all. They are types of mental mechanism which occur with great frequency in many " normal " people. Only in their more extreme manifestations do they become abnormal.

COMPENSATIONS

One of these is the mechanism of *compensation*. We have already mentioned Adler's theory in Chapter VII. The main idea which is relevant to our present purpose is that everybody attempts to compensate for a feeling of inferiority which arises in childhood when the child feels himself to be inferior to his parents and to the world at large because of his physical weakness and dependency. The feeling of inferiority is likely to be stronger than the average in children who are physically handicapped by deafness, a stutter, a club foot, etc. : it is also likely to occur in the unwanted child who may be made to feel his inferiority by his parents more than is the average child : or in a younger or youngest child : or again it may occur in a slightly different way in the spoilt child who, having everything provided for him in his home, never really finds his feet and consequently, when he

goes away from home and finds he is no longer so much the centre of attention as he was within it, develops a feeling of inferiority with its resulting compensatory behaviour.

These feelings of inferiority which all of us possess, though some possess more strongly than others, lead us to attempt compensations for them. And so long as the form of compensation we decide upon lies within our capacities we are able to remain in adjustment with our environment. If, however, we set our goal too high some form of maladjustment will develop. Now since different people possess different levels of ability, and since different people possess different depths of inferiority feeling, the compensations (often unrecognised for what they are by the individual who uses them) will differ both in kind and in degree. Some may be observed quite frequently in our friends or acquaintances (though it would be rash to conclude that every instance of the kind of behaviour about to be described is of necessity the result of compensation) ; others are observable in mental-hospital patients. Let us look at the types of behaviour which are often the result of compensating for some consciously or unconsciously recognised feeling of inferiority.

(a) Over-evaluation

One of the types goes by the name of *over-evaluation*. This may concern some physical or mental characteristic, or it may concern personal property. Thus, for example, a girl with pretty teeth may acquire ways of talking or of smiling or of laughing so that her teeth are shown off to the best advantage. One would not care to criticise this form of behaviour ; the girl may easily improve her social adjustment by adopting it. But if she were to practise ways of improving her smile in front of the mirror for most of the day, and if she did this to the neglect of other duties, then the behaviour would become a form of maladjustment. Another example of the same kind of behaviour would be a man who prided himself on his powers of observation, and who over-evaluated this characteristic to such a degree that he consistently led any conversation round, or broke into any discussion, so as to be able to demonstrate the fact that he had observed some perhaps rather insignificant and irrelevant detail.

Another example of over-evaluation lies in a person's attitude towards economic or social status. Because he over-values wealth or social class a person may tend to live beyond his income, buy the more expensive rather than the less expensive

things, recount stories about the behaviour of the aristocracy, and if possible any connection with them he may have had, and generally try to keep up appearances so as to impress his neighbours with his economic or social importance. " Keeping up with the Joneses ", social snobbery and other kinds of competitive emulation of the same general type may therefore frequently be regarded as manifestations of this mechanism of over-evaluation.

(b) *Introjection*

The next mechanism we shall consider goes by the name of *introjection*. It is closely related to the last example of over-evaluation. In this one tends to obtain reflected glory from some other person or group of people or even institution with whom one associates, or who possess some of the qualities which one admires. It may be shown in the pleasure which one member of a family experiences when another member achieves some success : or in the pleasure which is felt when one's school wins a game, or as part of the reaction when one's country wins a war : it may be shown, if one is a devoted conservative, in pleasure at being elected a member of the Carlton, or, if one is an intellectual, to the Athenæum, or, if one is a sportsman, to the M.C.C. It may be an alternative to over-evaluation in accounting for the pleasure some people might obtain from being seen walking down Bond Street with a duke on either arm, or at being seen lunching at the " Ivy " with a different girl every day, each one of them more attractive than the last.

In its more abnormal and extreme manifestations one comes to identify oneself to such a degree with another admired individual that one believes one is in fact that person himself. So one might actually believe oneself to be Napoleon or Frances Day or Lord Rothschild and behave in the way in which one believes they would behave.

(c) *Belittling Others*

So far we have considered mechanisms by which a person attempts to raise his own importance. But the end result is the same if instead of raising oneself one diminishes the importance of other people. There are a number of mechanisms of this type. One of the most frequent is to belittle them by fault-finding, destructive criticism and malicious gossip. The people who are the object of gossip are most frequently the superiors of the person who gossips about them, or else they are people of whom the person who gossips is jealous or envious in some

way. Thus gossip by students about members of their teaching staff may be attributable to envy of the position of superiority which the teachers enjoy, whereas gossip by members of the teaching staff about their students may be attributable to envy of the students' freedom and relative lack of responsibility.

(d) Projection

Another common mechanism goes by the name of *projection*. In this one tends to blame others for one's own failures and weaknesses and shortcomings. A person who is unconsciously aware of his own shortcomings sees them as if they appeared in another person. He criticises others for the faults he possesses himself. It is observable in a mild degree in many forms of behaviour, one of which might be the tendency of the incompetent car driver to complain of the bad manners of other road users. In more severe forms the mechanism gives rise to a delusional symptom, e.g. when an elderly spinster accuses a young doctor of making sexual advances to her.

A somewhat similar mechanism is to blame other people for one's own limitations, by pointing out that the pressure of social customs, traditions, conventions and other restrictions is so strong that it has prevented one from making a deeper mark on the world than one otherwise would have. Or to maintain that the workings of one's mind are really so far ahead of those of other people that they are unable to keep up with one and so fail to understand one's true worth. In more severe forms this mechanism may be seen in what are called *ideas of reference* and *ideas of influence*, that is to say, beliefs that people are making uncomplimentary remarks about one, that they are planning methods of encompassing one's discomfiture, or that they are forcing one to do things one does not want to do.

(e) Belittling Oneself

As a final example of these compensatory mechanisms may be mentioned the rather subtle technique of belittling oneself. It occurs with great frequency in ordinary life—though it is often a reflection of a genuine modesty and should not (any more than any of the other mechanisms that have been mentioned) inevitably be taken to indicate a compensatory mechanism at work. As examples of some common ways in which the mechanism may be used as a form of compensation we may take the not unusual apology for having played so badly which someone who has lost a game, e.g. of tennis, may make to his opponent,

or the apology which some speakers (or lecturers) not infrequently make for not having time to go into the subject in greater detail, or for having been hurried in preparation (by circumstances over which they have had no control), or for being poor at public speaking.   In these ways criticism may be disarmed, and perhaps even praise for what has been accomplished in spite of the difficulties may be awarded.   The apologies also tend to give the impression that the speaker (or lecturer) really knows far more about the subject than he has been able to say in his speech.

REPRESSION AND THE FREUDIAN THEORY

In all the mechanisms that have so far been mentioned (when, let it be said again, they are true examples of such mechanism) there is some degree of what is called *rationalisation*, that is to say the assignment of a false motive to behaviour because the person using the mechanism would be ashamed consciously to acknowledge the true motive.   The true motive is repressed into the unconscious mind.

The mechanism of *repression* is discussed at length in the picturesque analogy of the Freudian theory.[1]   According to this view every mental process belongs in the first place to the unconscious and from there it may, under certain conditions, proceed further into the conscious system.   Freud compares the unconscious system to a large ante-room in which the various mental excitations crowd upon one another like individual human beings at a popular reception.   Adjoining the ante-room is a second, smaller apartment, a sort of reception room in which consciousness resides.   But on the threshold between the two rooms there stands a doorkeeper, the *Censor*, who examines the various mental excitations that are struggling for admittance to the reception room, censors them and refuses them admittance if he disapproves of them.   He is a kind of Lord Chamberlain scrutinising the credentials of those who clamour to be presented at Court.   If he is very vigilant he will stop those he disapproves of at the threshold : if he is off his guard the mental excitations may temporarily slip into the reception room until he notices them and drives them out again.   But even those favoured mental excitations which are granted permission, or otherwise manage, to pass the threshold do not necessarily enter consciousness immediately.   They only do so if they succeed in attracting attention, much as, to change the analogy, a member of parlia-

[1] Freud (5), pp. 248–51.

ment is permitted to speak in debate only if he is successful in catching the eye of the Speaker. This second chamber is given the name of the *pre-conscious*. If the Censor refuses any mental excitation admittance to the pre-conscious system that mental excitation is *repressed*. Repression, however, does not destroy a mental excitation : the mental excitation remains in a condition of stress with its energy undischarged. It is consequently likely to appear again if it can elude the vigilance of the Censor, or if it can adopt some form that the Censor will not recognise.

The mental excitations which are most likely to be repressed are those which conflict with the system of morals and ideals which the individual has built up during his training and development, and which would therefore tend to lower his feeling of self-respect if he were to acknowledge their existence in an unmodified form. As one example we may take the attitude of *ambivalence* which some children (most, or all children according to Freud) may show towards their parents. They both love them and hate them. They love them for the care and protection, the food and the warmth they receive from them : they hate them for the restrictions which they necessarily impose upon them and for not allowing them to do everything they want to. The force of social conventions is such that they cannot (without losing self-respect) obviously betray these feelings of hostility. They therefore repress them and keep them repressed. It is sometimes possible, however, to show that a person's behaviour towards his parents rests on this unacknowledged and repressed antagonism towards them. A special form of this antagonism is the *Œdipus* complex and the *Electra* complex. In the Œdipus complex a son, through his more intimate association with his mother than with his father, is believed to fall in love with her and to hate his father for the rights he possesses over her. A similar situation exists in the daughter's corresponding attitude towards her father and her mother, although the development of the attitudes is rather more difficult to explain.

There is no doubt that in some cases the behaviour of sons towards their fathers and of daughters towards their mothers is bound up with a different degree of affection which they may feel towards their two parents. But that the mechanism is as universal as Freud believed is far more questionable, and its extension to explain phenomena such as religion (God being identified with the father) or nationalism (one's country being identified with one's mother) is much thinner still.

In so far as the moral training of different people is the same they will tend to repress the same kinds of things : in so far as it is different one person may repress a mental excitation that will be consciously acknowledged by another without any shock to his ethical standards.

But those that are repressed continue to try to enter consciousness, and they can only do so, as we have seen, if they manage to slip past the Censor. The best chance they have of doing this is if they appear as a *symptom*, that is to say a " cleverly chosen ambiguity which has one meaning to the conscious and quite a different meaning to the unconscious system ". Some of these symptoms have already been discussed in this chapter. Their task of eluding the vigilance of the Censor is made still easier if the Censor is off his guard as he is, for example, when the person is very tired or when he is asleep.

This leads us to consider some of the mechanisms which Freud believes are employed during sleep.[1] Dreams, he thinks, are in most cases the expression of unconscious wishes. The dream as we dream it and subsequently remember it possesses a *manifest content*, but in order to interpret its true significance we must discover its *latent content*. The manifest content represents the distortion that the repressed desires of the latent content have had to undergo in order to elude the Censor, and various mechanisms are employed to achieve this object. One of them is known as *displacement*. Things that in the latent content are really important emotionally may appear as very minor incidents in the manifest content : similarly, things that in the manifest content appear to be most important may be of only minor significance in the latent content. A second mechanism is *condensation*, in which several items of importance in the latent content are combined and blended together so as to appear as a single event in the manifest content. It is a process rather like a composite photograph in which the photographs of a number of people are taken on the same plate. The resulting picture represents none of them individually but is a blending of them all. A third mechanism is *dramatisation*. The events of significance in the latent content are dramatised and portrayed as if in a play. The dreamer is able to adopt a detached attitude towards the events that are occurring in his dream because they appear to him as if he were merely part of the audience watching a theatrical performance unfold. A fourth mechanism is

[1] Freud (4).

symbolisation.   Each element in the manifest content is a symbol which signifies and stands for something else in the latent content. Thus instead of dreaming of a male sexual organ one dreams of a gun or a pencil : instead of dreaming of a female sexual organ one dreams of a box or a bottle.   But again, the universal validity of the symbolical aspects of these objects would seem to be open to question.   For instance, it is maintained that a king in the manifest content represents the father in the latent content : it may do so in some cases, but in others it might merely mean that the dreamer has social aspirations.

After the sleeper wakes and attempts to recall his dream a further mechanism occurs which makes the dream still harder to interpret.   This is known as *secondary elaboration.*   The dream as it is dreamt is often illogical and disconnected and spasmodic. The process of secondary elaboration is to weave the various disconnected items together into a form which makes a more logically connected whole, in this way making the individual and really separate items more difficult to disentangle from one another.

In interpreting the dream the Analyst is allowed to make use of the principle of ambivalence.   In this connection it means that a symbol may, if it fits a patient's case better, be interpreted as standing not for what it usually does but for the opposite. Thus a dagger which would ordinarily be interpreted as referring to the male sexual organ may, if necessary, be interpreted as referring to the female.   This latitude allowed to the Analyst in the interpretation of his patients' dreams would appear to destroy any basis of scientific exactitude for the theory.   Analysts are, however, entirely unmoved by such criticism.   They point out that the system is not to be judged according to rules that are used in scientific investigation.   It has been evolved as a clinical rather than as a scientific method, and the basis of criticism must therefore rest on whether or not the system works, that is to say, on whether or not patients can be cured of their maladjustments.   This line of argument is not, however, very convincing. It would be possible, if Analysts were prepared to take the trouble, to record the precise conditions under which, let us say, a particular symbol had been successfully interpreted in one way and those in which it had been successfully interpreted in the other. And if the record were made sufficiently comprehensive and exhaustive it would be possible to apply the ordinary scientific criteria to the theory and investigate its degree of truth or falsity.

Still, however much one may question on the available evidence the claim for a universal validity of the doctrines, there is no doubt that the Analysts have brought to the forefront a number of important mental mechanisms which one should be aware of as methods which are sometimes employed by some people as means of dealing with their difficulties in adjustment.

REGRESSION, SUBLIMATION AND FIXATION

Before leaving the Freudian theory let us consider the mechanism known as *regression*. Freud believes that the *libido*, i.e. the energy underlying the sexual instincts, is directed towards different objects in the course of normal development. At first it finds expression through the mouth in the pleasure an infant obtains from sucking. As the infant grows up the libido is directed towards other objects until in the normal person it finally finds expression in direction towards a person of the opposite sex. If, however, in adult life the libido should require expression in a way that conflicts with the system of morals and ideals he has built up in the course of his development, then a situation of potential neurosis has arisen. One way in which this conflict may be solved, however, a solution which allows the individual to remain in a normally healthy mental state, is by means of *sublimation*. Freud holds that sexually impelled excitations are very plastic and that they are able to change their object very easily. Sublimation, therefore, occurs when the original object of the sexual impulse is abandoned and a new aim is adopted, an aim which is social rather than sexual in character, e.g. instead of trying to win the girl one tries to win the game.

If, however, no satisfactory alternative object can be found, if, that is to say, no sublimation can take place, the libido may *regress* to an earlier object : it may return to one of the stages through which it has already passed and be directed on to the object that is characteristic of that phase. Regression is particularly likely to occur if the development of the libido has not been normal, for it is always possible that a part of the libido may become *fixated* on to the object characteristic of any phase and leave less to go on to the next stage. If this occurs it is easier for regression to occur when a person encounters a difficulty in adult life than if the development of the libido has been normal.

If regression does take place there are two ways in which the individual may react. He may consciously accept the regression because he sees nothing wrong in it, and it does not infringe his

conscience or conflict with his system of morals and ideals (due perhaps to having been brought up in a morally lax or in an unconventional environment). Thus he may consciously accept, let us say, homosexuality and actively live the life of a homosexual. This type of reaction is called a *perversion* and no neurosis necessarily arises. The individual continues to live his way of life and is relatively satisfied by it, although a neurosis may develop *indirectly* later if he finds he is ostracised by others because of his perversion.

The second way in which he may react is by means of repression, and a great effort will be expended to prevent the regression or fixation from entering consciousness. He may exhibit a whole host of symptoms and unusual types of behaviour, none of which he appreciates as being connected with a regression and repression, but which if unwoven could be shown to be caused by them. A regression (or fixation) together with repression invariably leads to a neurosis.

Now without fully accepting the whole of Freud's elaborate doctrine it is possible occasionally to see types of behaviour which may conveniently be classed as regressions. They are exhibited by people who refuse to be their age, who giggle for no discoverable reason, and who perform other types of immature behaviour which is more characteristic of people considerably younger than they. It is also shown by people who adopt stereotyped reactions in their dealings with other people, reactions which perhaps they have adopted as the result of seeing them frequently portrayed on the movies and which they believe to be characteristic of the behaviour of men and women. They sometimes occur in methods and manners of speech, e.g. the adoption of child-like turns of phrase that are unconsciously calculated to arouse protectiveness in other people, and they occur in other mechanisms of a similar kind as well. In an extreme form this mechanism is exhibited by the officer who was taken prisoner in the last war in circumstances in which he might justifiably have been accused of cowardice. He regressed psychologically to the age of five years. " He called the servants by the names which had belonged to servants who had been in the house when he was five. He called his young sister by the name of his eldest sister, etc. His speech was infantile. He lisped and used phrases and recalled incidents that his mother remembered only with difficulty." [1]

[1] Fisher (3), p. 96.

Persistent Non-adaptive Reactions

There remain to be considered a few more mechanisms which may arise in circumstances in which an individual is experiencing some difficulties in adjustment. One way of reacting to such a situation is to repeat and to persevere with the same type of behaviour over and over again, never getting any nearer the solution of the difficulty. The particular reaction is ineffective, but it is nevertheless repeated. If one arrives at a railway station at the end of a journey and unsuccessfully searches one's pockets for one's ticket, this type of reaction would be exhibited if one proceeded to search the same pockets over and over again. The more frequently one searches the same pockets without success the more emotional the situation is likely to become. It is true that a certain amount of persistence in the same type of behaviour is often quite useful socially. It may be illustrated by the effect which the spider had on Robert the Bruce, and, with less dramatic results, in the advantage which a research worker or a bank clerk obtains through possessing the characteristic in more than an average degree. But the type of persistence exhibited by the person who has lost his ticket is of a rather different kind : it is guided by emotion rather than by reason and so it becomes uneconomical and disturbing. In more extreme forms emotion and persistence are tied up together in obsessional and compulsive acts. These occur frequently in their milder forms among normal people, but the degree of emotion that accompanies a ritualistic act such as throwing spilt salt over the left shoulder or not walking under a ladder is rarely sufficiently strong to induce any feeling of worry if they are not indulged in, though there may be a slight *malaise*. These superstitions, too, depend on the current beliefs in the particular community in which the person is living. But the obsessions which make the patient so worried as to lead to an interference with his normal life are mainly those that do not have the backing of social acceptance and approval. They have been classified by Mapother and Lewis [1] into four types, though there is a good deal of overlap between the types, (1) Ideas and images, (2) Impulses, (3) Phobias, (4) Ruminations. An obsessional idea is a form of delusion : an obsessional impulse ranges from the minor ritualistic acts we have already mentioned up to a continual washing of the hands or to an impulse to plunge a knife into people on

[1] Mapother and Lewis (9), p. 1880.

the street : phobias take many forms ; some are irrational fears of, e.g. spiders, mice or cows, others are fears of open or enclosed spaces and so on : ruminations take the form of continual and pointless questioning or search, such as trying to recall a particular incident or name when there is no need to do so.

ANXIETIES AND OTHER EMOTIONAL OVER-REACTIONS

In the obsessions and compulsions the patient realises the incongruity of his actions and he is consequently upset because he feels he has to perform them. In other types of reaction he is not upset by having to do what he does, but by what he regards as the seriousness of his situation. His response is excessive and much stronger than the situation warrants, and it is often displaced on to objects other than the one which originally gave rise to the feeling. Typical of this reaction is anxiety. In both its milder forms of undue anxiety and in its more severe forms of anxiety neurosis the feeling is most likely to arise when a person feels his security is threatened. It is frequently found, too, to be associated with an inferiority feeling. After a person has been unsuccessful at something he has tried to do he may develop an attitude of self-depreciation, tend to undervalue his assets and to convince himself that he will be unsuccessful in any attempt to solve a subsequent difficulty of the same sort, even before he has begun to try. From this may follow the fear of encountering such difficulties, and, by extension, of encountering *any* difficulty. The anxiety neurotic is uneasy, and his thinking is spasmodic and disconnected. He is restless in his activity, but simultaneously shows symptoms of fatigue. Normal individuals sometimes show such symptoms, but in their case there is what we consider to be a more adequate predisposing cause—sometimes a completely adequate predisposing cause.

So, too, with other types of emotional reaction than anxiety. On coming into a fortune of several thousand pounds the normal person may be found to be vivacious and energetic, in constant high spirits and easily distractible. His constant high spirits may lead him to exaggerate and to distort, and everything he does, even the most irrelevant of his actions, may be carried out with zest and enthusiasm. This picture, too, is found in the manic patient in the mental hospital, but whereas with the normal person the phase of elation will be of only relatively brief duration, the manic patient's elation and euphoria will continue for a longer time and will prevent him from carrying on his life

in the ordinary way. It will not matter to the person who has inherited several thousand pounds if his elation incapacitates him temporarily from earning his own living, but in the case of the manic patient it usually matters very much.

In contrast to this picture of elation we have a completely different pattern of behaviour in depression. Here we find an over-reaction of quite a different type. Instead of being joyous and elated and vivacious the picture is one of gloom and misery. The actions are slow. The patient may sit for hours in the most profound dejection. He may, if he is willing to talk at all, say he has nothing to live for and that suicide is the only solution to his misery. The pattern may occur as a temporary phenomenon in the normal person who has suffered some severe emotional experience : in the mental-hospital patient, however, it is of much longer duration and there may be no discoverable adequate predisposing cause. Yet, if he is accessible to questions, he may mention the imaginary sins he has committed and the punishment that will be the just reward for his wickedness.

HYSTERIA AND INACCESSIBILITY

Finally there is a third technique which may be employed. Instead of worrying about the incongruity of his actions, or instead of over-reacting to the situation, a person may exhibit an under-reaction, apathy or indifference to his symptoms. In the normal person a more than usual degree of apathy may be partly, no doubt, due to the type of training he has received. Thus the Public School boy in England or the Plains Indian in America are noted for their reserve : the Sicilian for his lack of it. In those Englishmen who are trained to suppress the expression of emotion it would be wrong to infer that they do not feel emotional. Yet there are some quite normal people who do in fact feel less strongly than others in certain situations. In the abnormal individual we find apparent indifference and under-reaction in the maladjustment which is called hysteria. The hysteric is not upset by his reactions nor worried because he feels he has to do them. He accepts and discusses his symptoms in an emotionally detached way. His symptoms may take the form of an anæsthesia, a paralysis, a tremor, an amnesia,[1] a fugue,[2] as well as many others. They frequently occur after an industrial accident, and when they do so they complicate the physical results of the accident and tend to persist until the question of

---

[1] Loss of memory.   [2] See Chapter IV, pp. 54–5.

L

compensation has been settled. But whatever particular type of symptom may be shown it is the patient's indifference to his incapacitation that is one of the most noticeable features.

An exaggerated form of this inaccessibility and indifference is to be found in some types of *schizophrenia*. Major catastrophes may go on in the outside world, but the schizophrenic appears unmoved. If he has a system of delusions of persecution he may mention the depths of infamy to which his persecutors are descending with hardly as much as a conventional expression of annoyance.[1] Sometimes he will merely sit in a corner by himself or spend his day staring out of the window with a far-away expression on his face, apparently day-dreaming, and completely indifferent to his personal appearance. Sometimes he may seem to be quite normal, and it is only on getting to know him a little better that something " peculiar " is noticed about his behaviour. In this type of reaction we are approaching perhaps the man-in-the-street's picture of a don in one of the older universities.

WATSON'S THEORY OF EMOTION

Thus many of the types of reaction which are considered to be abnormal in our culture are to be found occasionally in those who are generally considered to be normal. The main difference between the abnormal's responses and those of the normal individual is that we consider the former's to be excessive or incongruous or too prolonged or inadequate—to be, in fact, out of proportion to what we consider to be the seriousness of the situation. The kind of situation in which normal emotion is likely to arise is that in which a person finds himself in a new or unexpected situation. This is the kind of situation that gives rise to difficulties, and the resulting maladjustment may be mild and lead to only transient emotional behaviour or more severe and give rise to a more prolonged type of maladjustment.

It has been the view of some authorities that human beings possess a few innate patterns of emotional reaction, and that all the varied forms of emotional expression that one encounters among adults are modified from these few. Thus Watson [2] thought that all emotions except three were conditioned reflexes based on the conditioning of responses to the three unconditioned emotional reactions of fear, rage and love. He thought that

[1] This is not true of all schizophrenics, for some types tend to over-react unexpectedly for very minor reasons.
[2] Watson (12), Chap. 7.

these unconditioned emotional reactions could be evoked in the young infant in the following ways : For *fear*, a loud sound or a sudden loss of support ; for *rage*, hampering of movement, e.g. when the arms were kept pressed against the sides ; for *love*, stroking the skin, tickling, gentle rocking or patting, or the stimulation of the erogenous zones. All the other emotional reactions he considered to be conditioned to these three. For example, Watson conditioned fear in an infant to a white rat by striking a bar behind the infant's head as he stretched his hand out to feel the rat. When the fear response had been conditioned to the rat it extended itself to other furry animals which previously called out neither a positive nor a negative response. Furthermore, by presenting the animal at meal-times, Watson found that it was possible to uncondition the fear response, so that the infant once more stretched out his hand to feel the rat. Watson maintained that other emotional reactions become conditioned or unconditioned in a similar way.

The generalisation of the theory is, however, farfetched. To prove that some emotional reactions can be conditioned does not prove that they all are conditioned : again, the conditioned fear experiment does not succeed with all infants ; some turn round and scowl at the loud noise and do not appear to connect it with the white rat. Furthermore, the results of Sherman's experiment do not support the theory.

Sherman [1] used infants below 12 days old in his experiment and gave the following four different types of stimuli : (1) *Hunger*, the infants being kept fifteen minutes beyond their usual feeding time ; (2) *Dropping* them 2 to 3 feet towards a table ; (3) *Restraint*, the infant's head and face being held down on the table with a fairly firm pressure ; (4) *Pricking* their cheeks six times with a needle. Sherman divided his observers into four groups : (*a*) One group was shown motion pictures of the stimulating circumstances and the ensuing responses ; (*b*) A second group was shown the motion pictures of the ensuing responses without being shown the stimulating circumstances ; (*c*) A third group was shown the film in which the stimuli and responses were transposed, e.g. pricking with the needle being shown before the response to restraint, and so on ; (*d*) A fourth group had direct observation of the infants' responses, but the stimuli were applied while the infants were behind a screen. The observers in this group, therefore, had to depend on their

[1] Sherman (11).

observation of behaviour without knowing the stimulating circumstances.

The results were that 27 of the 40 observers in group (a) answered " fear " to the dropping, 24 named " anger " to the restraint, 13 answered " pain " to the sticking with a needle, and 7 named " hunger " to the missing of the meal. Furthermore, eighteen of the observers stated that they named the various emotions they did because they were influenced by seeing the stimuli. In group (b) the judgments of the emotions were very variable : anger was given most frequently—11 times to the hunger reaction, 14 times to the dropping reaction, 13 times to the behaviour following restraint, and 8 times to the behaviour following pricking with a needle. A similar discrepancy was found in the interpretation of other types of behaviour. As an instance of the difference between groups (a) and (b) may be mentioned the fact that of the observers in group (b) only 15 per cent. attributed the response of fear to the dropping, while in group (a) 67 per cent. did.

In the case of group (c), when the anger reaction was preceded by a leader representing fifteen minutes' delay of feeding, 60 per cent. named hunger as the reaction, and when the hunger reaction was preceded by the restraint 46 per cent. named anger as the reaction. By pure chance one would expect such estimations in only 25 per cent. of the cases. Thus the stimulus preceding the reaction was usually the deciding factor in the name given to the reaction.

In the case of group (d) " colic " was most frequently suggested as the cause of all the responses. The observers in this group were mostly medical students, so they may have judged by inference. The nurses in the group, too, tended to say that the behaviour was due either to colic or to being awakened from sleep. The decisions, therefore, appear to have been based on *probability* rather than on differential observation.

Thus these heartless experiments indicated that there is no pattern of expression which may be said to characterise any particular emotion. Yet if, as Watson maintained, there are three innate patterns of emotional response—fear, anger and love—then Sherman ought to have found a large percentage of agreement among the judges naming the reactions. Whether the reaction was named rage, fear or love does not matter very much. The point is that they should have fallen into three clearly marked groups. In fact they did not do so. Sherman's

work shows that the differentiations of the infants' responses are made on the basis of responses to given stimulating conditions, and they are only accurate when these stimulating conditions are known.

DARWIN'S THEORY OF EMOTION

Darwin's [1] theory of the fundamental nature of emotional expression was in some ways even wider than Watson's. Darwin formulated three principles :

(1) *The Principle of Serviceable Associated Habits.* This is that certain actions and movements are useful in order to relieve certain sensations of desires, and that these actions may become associated by habit with the sensations. They may, according to Darwin, persist even after their original usefulness has passed, and as an example he mentions that he found it impossible to stop himself from leaping backwards when a poisonous snake in the Zoo struck at him from the other side of the glass through which he was observing it. Another example of the same kind of thing is the behaviour of a dog turning round and round before lying down on the drawing-room carpet, a habit which has persisted from the time when the dog in the prairie turned round and round on the grass before lying down, in order to prepare a comfortable place on which to rest.

(2) *The Principle of Antithesis.* According to the first principle certain states of mind lead to the establishment of certain habitual actions. Therefore, according to Darwin, when a directly opposite state of mind exists an opposite set of reactions will occur. For example,

> When a dog approaches a strange dog or man in a savage or hostile frame of mind, he walks upright and very stiffly ; his head is slightly raised, or not much lowered ; the tail is held erect and quite rigid ; the hairs bristle, especially along the neck and back ; the pricked ears are directed forwards, and the eyes have a fixed stare. These actions . . . follow from the dog's intention to attack his enemy, and are thus to a large extent intelligible . . . Let us now suppose that the dog suddenly discovers that the man whom he is approaching is not a stranger, but his master ; and let it be observed how completely and instantaneously his whole bearing is reversed. Instead of walking upright, the body sinks downwards or even crouches, and is thrown into flexuous movements ; his tail, instead of being held stiff and upright, is lowered and wagged from side to side ; his hair instantly becomes smooth ; his ears are depressed and drawn backwards, but not closely to

[1] Darwin (1)

the head ; and his lips hang loosely. From the drawing back of
the ears, the eyelids become elongated, and the eyes no longer
appear round and staring. . . . Not one of the above movements,
so completely expressive of affection, are of the least direct service
to the animal. They are explicable, as far as I can see, solely
from being in complete opposition or antithesis to the attitude
and movements which, from intelligible causes, are assumed
when a dog intends to fight, and which consequently are expressive of anger.[1]

Similarly, the serviceable associated habit of the frowning
brow, thrown-back shoulders and clenched fists expressive of
rage and power has as its antithesis the raised eyebrows, shrugging
shoulders and open palms expressive of impotence, or the
inability to cope with a situation.

(3) *The Direct Action of the Nervous System.* According to
Darwin's third principle, when an individual is strongly excited
nervous energy is released and finds expression by means of
movements which partly depend on nervous connections and
partly on habit. For example, when we are terribly afraid, the
excess nervous energy finds its expression in trembling ; when
we are in agony we writhe ; when we are in pain we perspire ;
when we are enraged we clench and grind the teeth, heave the
chest, and so on.

Now according to Darwin's principles and the elaboration
he makes of them, each and every kind of emotion is represented
by different and specific kinds of expressive movements. Therefore it ought to follow, if this is true, that one can accurately
describe the emotions depicted if one sees photographs of people
expressing various emotions. But the experimental work that has
been done on this point is far from convincing.

In the first place there have been experiments in which
photographs or artists' sketches of posed emotional expressions
have been used. Feleky,[2] for example, posed for a series of
photographs over a period of about a year, endeavouring to
depict various emotions. Similarly, Langfeld [3] used artists'
sketches of posed emotional expressions. These photographs or
artists' sketches were then shown to a group of individuals who
were asked to indicate the particular emotion that was portrayed
on each. It was found that there was considerable uncertainty
in the judgment of many of the photographs and sketches, some
being judged relatively accurately, others very poorly. One
reason for this might, of course, be that the emotions depicted

[1] Darwin, pp. 50-1.   [2] Feleky (2).   [3] Langfeld (8).

were posed, and that people who posed were not actually in the emotional situation at the time. Consequently they might exaggerate traditional or conventional expressions rather than modes of expression used in actual emotional situations. Landis,[1] therefore, photographed people (unknown to them) while they were actually exhibiting emotion : but he found no characteristic pattern for each emotion, and no better agreement about the emotions being experienced when the photographs were shown to other people for judgment than was found with the posed photographs or the artists' sketches.

These facts seem to indicate, therefore, that our judgments in ordinary life must be based on some other factor, for there is little doubt that in ordinary life we are able to interpret with fair accuracy the emotion that an individual is experiencing. This additional factor is the total situation in which the person happens to be at the time, or which we believe him to be in. The results of Sherman's experiments have already shown us the importance of this factor.

CULTURAL PATTERNING OF EMOTIONAL EXPRESSION

Another deduction from Darwin's theory would be that all people, including primitive people, should express the same emotion in the same way. This can be investigated by referring to anthropological material.[2] Thus Darwin regarded the shake of the head from side to side to mean " No " as an extension of the child's refusal of food. Yet he himself pointed out that this was by no means a universal behaviour pattern. Thus the Dyaks of Borneo contract their eyebrows slightly to mean " No ", the Sicilians raise the head and chin, and so on.

Tears, too, do not always imply sorrow. It is reported that among the Maori of New Zealand no demonstration was made on the departure of a friend, but tears were shed if he returned. And even when they are used to imply grief there is often a conventional pattern—thus in China it is reported that the amount of emotional display permitted on a sorrowful occasion depended on a person's social class. A nobleman showed less emotion than a commoner, and for the latter to be restrained implied that he was presuming beyond his class.

Again, in Western culture it is conventional to stand up in the presence of a superior as a mark of respect. But the inhabi-

---

[1] Landis (7).
[2] See Klineberg (6) for a fuller account of the examples given below.

tants of Fiji or the Tonga Islands sit down in those circumstances. The inhabitants of the Friendly Islands take off their clothes as a mark of respect, and the Todas raise the open right hand to the face, resting the thumb on the bridge of the nose. To us it means something rather different from respect.

The causes of emotion may also vary. Some authorities have endeavoured to explain shame on a sexual basis, but there are many groups who go about without any clothes, or who wear clothes which cover parts of the body which we do not regard it as shameful to conceal, while leaving other more intimate parts of their bodies unclothed. There are groups of Australians who feel most ashamed when they are not wearing their nose ring—the sole article of clothing they wear. Similarly, too, death is not always regarded as a cause of sorrow : to some peoples it is accepted with rejoicing.

Thus it follows that the cultural pattern very largely determines the kind of emotion, the amount of emotion, and the way the emotion is expressed in different situations. It is not surprising, in view of this, that when we try to judge emotional expression from photographs we should be so unreliable, for in ordinary life we are guided by the total situation that the individual happens to be in at the time, and when we see people exhibiting emotional behaviour in real life we do not judge so much by their muscles and expressions as by the situation they are in. It is quite possible to infer entirely the wrong emotions if we apply the conventions of our own culture to the behaviour of people in another. Thus Porteus,[1] on asking a group of Australian natives to do a particular dance for him, was met with a volley of replies, apparently in terms of the most vehement refusal. He felt that the language needed no interpretation. Nevertheless, his interpreter remarked that they were saying that they would do it for him. Every cultural pattern has its own types of response which it considers to be normal and others which it considers to be abnormal. Not only so, but in addition a type which is considered to be abnormal by one culture may be the most ordinary and usual pattern of response in another.

[1] Porteus (10).

REFERENCES

1. DARWIN, C., *Expression of Emotion in Animals and Men*. London : Murray, 1872, pp. 374.

2. FELEKY, A. M., " The expression of emotions ". *Psychol. Rev.*, 1934, **21**, 33–41.

3. FISHER, V. E., *An Introduction to Abnormal Psychology*. New York : Macmillan, 1931, pp. 512.

4. FREUD, S., *Interpretation of Dreams*. London : Allen & Unwin, 1937, revised edn., pp. 600.

5. ——, *Introductory Lectures on Psycho-analysis*. London : Allen & Unwin, 2nd edn., 1943, pp. 395.

6. KLINEBERG, O., *Race Differences*. New York : Harper, 1935, pp. 366.

7. LANDIS, C., " The Interpretation of Facial Expression in Emotion ". *J. General Psychol.*, 1929, **2**, 59–72.

8. LANGFELD, H. S., " The Judgment of Emotion by Facial Expression ". *J. Abn. Psychol.*, 1918, **13**, 171–84.

9. MAPOTHER, E., and LEWIS, A. J., " Psychological Medicine ". Sect. 21 of *A Textbook of the Practice of Medicine* (Ed., F. W. Price). Oxford : University Press, 6th edn., 1941, pp. 2032.

10. PORTEUS, S. D. *The Psychology of a Primitive People*. London : Arnold, 1931, pp. 438.

11. SHERMAN, M., " The Differentiation of Emotional Responses in Infants." *J. Comp. Psychol.*, 1928, **7**, 265–84, 335–51.

12. WATSON, J. B., *Behaviorism*. London : Kegan Paul, 1931, pp. 308.

INDEX OF AUTHORITIES

INDEX OF SUBJECTS

The International Library of
Sociology
and Social Reconstruction

Edited by W. J. H. SPROTT
Founded by KARL MANNHEIM

ROUTLEDGE & KEGAN PAUL
BROADWAY HOUSE, CARTER LANE, LONDON, E.C.4

CONTENTS

PRINTED IN GREAT BRITAIN BY HEADLEY BROTHERS LTD
109 KINGSWAY LONDON WC2 AND ASHFORD KENT

GENERAL SOCIOLOGY

Gibson, Quentin. The Logic of Social Enquiry. *240 pp. 1960. 24s.*

Goldschmidt, Professor Walter. Understanding Human Society. *272 pp. 1959. 21s.*

Johnson, Harry M. Sociology: a Systematic Introduction. *Foreword by Robert K. Merton. 710 pp. 1961. (2nd Impression 1962.) 42s.*

Mannheim, Karl. Essays on Sociology and Social Psychology. *Edited by Paul Keckskemeti. With Editorial Note by Adolph Lowe. 344 pp. 1953. 30s.*
Systematic Sociology: An Introduction to the Study of Society. *Edited by J. S. Erös and Professor W. A. C. Stewart. 220 pp. 1957. (2nd Impression 1959.) 24s.*

Martindale, Don. The Nature and Types of Sociological Theory. *292 pp. 1961. 35s.*

Maus, Heinz. A Short History of Sociology. *234 pp. 1962. 28s.*

Myrdal, Gunnar. Value in Social Theory: A Collection of Essays on Methodology. *Edited by Paul Streeten. 332 pp. 1958. (2nd Impression 1962.) 32s.*

Ogburn, William F., and **Nimkoff, Meyer F.** A Handbook of Sociology. *Preface by Karl Mannheim. 612 pp. 46 figures. 38 tables. 4th edition (revised) 1960. 35s.*

Parsons, Talcott and **Smelser, Neil J.** Economy and Society: A Study in the Integration of Economic and Social Theory. *362 pp. 1956. (2nd Impression 1957.) 35s.*

Rex, John. Key Problems of Sociological Theory. *220 pp. 1961. 25s.*

FOREIGN CLASSICS OF SOCIOLOGY

Durkheim, Emile. Suicide. A Study in Sociology. *Edited and with an Introduction by George Simpson. 404 pp. 1952. 30s.*
Socialism and Saint-Simon. *Edited with an Introduction by Alvin W. Gouldner. Translated by Charlotte Sattler from the edition originally edited with an Introduction by Marcel Mauss. 286 pp. 1959. 28s.*
Professional Ethics and Civic Morals. *Translated by Cornelia Brookfield. 288 pp. 1957. 30s.*

Gerth, H. H., and **Wright Mills, C.** From Max Weber: Essays in Sociology. *502 pp. 1948. (4th Impression 1961.) 32s.*

Tönnies, Ferdinand. Community and Association. *(Gemeinschaft und Gesellschaft.) Translated and Supplemented by Charles P. Loomis. Foreword by Pitirim A. Sorokin. 334 pp. 1955. 25s.*

SOCIAL STRUCTURE

Andrzejewski, Stanislaw. Military Organization and Society. *With a Foreword by Professor A. R. Radcliffe-Brown. 226 pp. 1 folder. 1954. 21s.*

Cole, G. D. H. Studies in Class Structure. *220 pp. 1955. (2nd Impression 1961.) 21s.*

Coontz, Sydney H. Population Theories and the Economic Interpretation. *202 pp. 1957. (2nd Impression 1961.) 25s.*

Coser, Lewis. The Functions of Social Conflict. *204 pp. 1956. 18s.*

Eisenstadt, S. N. From Generation to Generation: Age Groups and Social Structure. *374 pp. 1956. 42s.*

Kelsall, R. K. Higher Civil Servants in Britain: From 1870 to the Present Day. *268 pp. 31 tables. 1955. 25s.*

Marsh, David C. The Changing Social Structure of England and Wales, 1871-1951. *296 pp. 63 tables. 1958. 28s.*

SOCIOLOGY AND POLITICS

Barbu, Zevedei. Democracy and Dictatorship: Their Psychology and Patterns of Life. *300 pp. 1956. 28s.*

Benney, Mark, Gray, A. P., and Pear, R. H. How People Vote: a Study of Electoral Behaviour in Greenwich. *Foreword by Professor W. A. Robson. 256 pp. 70 tables. 1956. 25s.*

Bramstedt, Dr. E. K. Dictatorship and Political Police: The Technique of Control by Fear. *286 pp. 1945. 20s.*

Crick, Bernard. The American Science of Politics: Its Origins and Conditions. *284 pp. 1959. 28s.*

Hertz, Frederick. Nationality in History and Politics: A Psychology and Sociology of National Sentiment and Nationalism. *440 pp. 1944. (4th Impression 1957.) 32s.*

Kornhauser, William. The Politics of Mass Society. *272 pp. 20 tables. 1960. 25s.*

Laidler, Harry W. Social-Economic Movements: An Historical and Comparative Survey of Socialism, Communism, Co-operation, Utopianism; and other Systems of Reform and Reconstruction. *864 pp. 16 plates. 1 figure. 1949. (3rd Impression 1960.) 50s.*

Mannheim, Karl. Freedom, Power and Democratic Planning. *Edited by Hans Gerth and Ernest K. Bramstedt. 424 pp. 1951. 35s.*

Myrdal, Gunnar. The Political Element in the Development of Economic Theory. *Translated from the German by Paul Streeten. 282 pp. 1953. (3rd Impression 1961.) 25s.*

Polanyi, Michael, F.R.S. The Logic of Liberty: Reflections and Rejoinders. *228 pp. 1951. 18s.*

Verney, Douglas V. The Analysis of Political Systems. *264 pp. 1959. (2nd Impression 1961.) 28s.*

FOREIGN AFFAIRS: THEIR SOCIAL, POLITICAL AND ECONOMIC FOUNDATIONS

Bonné, Alfred. The Economic Development of the Middle East: An Outline of Planned Reconstruction after the War. *192 pp. 58 tables. 1945. (3rd Impression 1953.) 16s.*
State and Economics in the Middle East: A Society in Transition. *482 pp. 2nd (revised) edition 1955. (2nd Impression 1960.) 40s.*
Studies in Economic Development: with special reference to Conditions in the Under-developed Areas of Western Asia and India. *322 pp. 84 tables. (2nd edition 1960.) 32s.*

Douglas, Dorothy W. Transitional Economic Systems. The Polish-Czech Example. *384 pp. 1953. 25s.*

Hughes, Everett C. French Canada in Transition. *252 pp. 49 tables. 16 figures. 4 maps. 1946. 16s.*

Mayer, J. P. Political Thought in France from the Revolution to the Fifth Republic. *164 pp. 3rd edition (revised) 1961. 16s.*

Schenk, H. G. The Aftermath of the Napoleonic Wars: The Concert of Europe—an Experiment. *250 pp. 17 plates. 1947. 18s.*

Schlesinger, Rudolf. Central European Democracy and its Background: Economic and Political Group Organization. *432 pp. 1953. 30s.*

Thomson, David, Meyer, E., and Briggs, A. Patterns of Peacemaking. *408 pp. 1945. 25s.*

Trouton, Ruth. Peasant Renaissance in Yugoslavia, 1900-1950: A Study of the Development of Yugoslav Peasant Society as affected by Education. *370 pp. 1 map. 1952. 28s.*

SOCIOLOGY OF LAW

Gurvitch, Dr. Georges. Sociology of Law. *With a Preface by Professor Roscoe Pound. 280 pp. 1947. (2nd Impression 1953.) 24s.*

Renner, Karl. The Institutions of Private Law and Their Social Functions. *Edited, with an Introduction and Notes by O. Kahn-Freund. Translated by Agnes Schwarzschild. 336 pp. 1949. 28s.*

CRIMINOLOGY

Cloward, Richard A., and Ohlin, Lloyd E. Delinquency and Opportunity: A Theory of Delinquent Gangs. *248 pp. 1961. 25s.*

Friedländer, Dr. Kate. The Psycho-Analytical Approach to Juvenile Delinquency: Theory, Case Studies, Treatment. *320 pp. 1947. (5th Impression 1961.) 25s.*

Glueck, Sheldon and Eleanor. Family Environment and Delinquency. *With the statistical assistance of Rose W. Kneznek. 340 pp. 1962. 35s.*

Grygier, Tadeusz. Oppression: a Study in Social and Criminal Psychology. *Foreword by Hermann Mannheim. 392 pp. 1954. 28s.*

Mannheim, Hermann. Group Problems in Crime and Punishment, and other Studies in Criminology and Criminal Law. *336 pp. 1955. 28s.*

Morris, Terence. The Criminal Area: A Study in Social Ecology. *Foreword by Hermann Mannheim. 232 pp. 25 tables. 4 maps. 1957. 25s.*

Spencer, John C. Crime and the Services. *Foreword by Hermann Mannheim. 336 pp. 1954. 28s.*

Trasler, Gordon. The Explanation of Criminality. *144 pp. 1962. 20s.*

SOCIAL PSYCHOLOGY

Barbu, Zevedei. Problems of Historical Psychology. *248 pp. 1960. 25s.*

Blackburn, Julian. Psychology and the Social Pattern. *184 pp. 1945. (6th Impression 1961.) 16s.*
The Framework of Human Behaviour. *182 pp. 1947. (2nd Impression 1953.) 15s.*

Fleming, C. M. Adolescence: Its Social Psychology: With an Introduction to recent findings from the fields of Anthropology, Physiology, Medicine, Psychometrics and Sociometry. *288 pp. (2nd edition 1962.) 18s.*
The Social Psychology of Education: An Introduction and Guide to Its Study. *136 pp. (2nd edition (revised) 1959.) 11s.*

Fleming, C. M. (Ed.). Studies in the Social Psychology of Adolescence. *Contributions by J. E. Richardson, J. F. Forrester, J. K. Shukla and P. J. Higginbotham. Foreword by the editor. 292 pp. 29 figures. 13 tables. 5 folder tables. 1951. 23s.*

Halmos, Paul. Solitude and Privacy: a Study of Social Isolation, its Causes and Therapy. *With a Foreword by Professor T. H. Marshall. 216 pp. 1952. 21s.*
Towards a Measure of Man: The Frontiers of Normal Adjustment. *276 pp. 1957. 28s.*

Hollitscher, Walter. Sigmund Freud: An Introduction. A Presentation of his Theory, and a Discussion of the Relationship between Psycho-Analysis and Sociology. *140 pp. 1947. (2nd Impression 1950.) 12s.*

Homans, George C. The Human Group. *Foreword by Bernard DeVoto. Introduction by Robert K. Merton. 526 pp. 1951. (3rd Impression 1959.) 28s.*
Social Behaviour: its Elementary Forms. *416 pp. 1961. 30s.*

Klein, Josephine. The Study of Groups. *226 pp. 31 figures. 5 tables. 1956. (3rd Impression 1962.) 21s.*

Linton, Ralph. The Cultural Background of Personality. *132 pp. 1947. (4th Impression 1958.) 16s.*
See also Yang, M.

Mayo, Elton. The Social Problems of an Industrial Civilization. With an appendix on the Political Problem. *180 pp. 1949. (4th Impression 1961.) 15s.*

Ridder, J. C. de. The Personality of the Urban African in South Africa. A Thematic Apperception Test Study. *196 pp. 12 plates. 1961. 25s.*

Rose, Arnold M. (Ed.). Mental Health and Mental Disorder: A Sociological Approach. *Chapters by 46 contributors. 654 pp. 1956. 40s.*
Human Behavior and Social Processes: an Interactionist Approach. *Contributions by Arnold M. Ross, Ralph H. Turner, Anselm Strauss, Everett C. Hughes, E. Franklin Frazier, Howard S. Becker, et al. 696 pp. 1962. 56s.*

Spinley, Dr. B. M. The Deprived and the Privileged: Personality Development in English Society. *232 pp. 1953. 20s.*

Wolfenstein, Martha. Disaster: A Psychological Essay. *264 pp. 1957. 23s.*

Young, Professor Kimball. Personality and Problems of Adjustment. *742 pp. 12 figures. 9 tables. 2nd edition (revised) 1952. (2nd Impression 1959.) 40s.*
Handbook of Social Psychology. *658 pp. 16 figures. 10 tables. 2nd edition (revised) 1957. (2nd Impression 1960.) 35s.*

SOCIOLOGY OF THE FAMILY

Banks, J. A. Prosperity and Parenthood: A Study of Family Planning among the Victorian Middle Classes. *262 pp. 1954. 24s.*

Chapman, Dennis. The Home and Social Status. *336 pp. 8 plates. 3 figures. 117 tables. 1955. 35s.*

Folsom, Joseph K. The Family and Democratic Society. *With chapters in collaboration with Marion Bassett. 782 pp. 1948. 35s.*

Klein, Viola. The Feminine Character: History of an Ideology. *With a Foreword by Karl Mannheim. 256 pp. 1946. 16s.*

Myrdal, Alva and Klein, Viola. Women's Two Roles: Home and Work. *238 pp. 27 tables. 1956. 25s.*

Parsons, Talcott and Bales, Robert F. Family: Socialization and Interaction Process. *In collaboration with James Olds, Morris Zelditch and Philip E. Slater. 456 pp. 50 figures and tables. 1956. 35s.*

THE SOCIAL SERVICES

Ashdown, Margaret and Brown, S. Clement. Social Service and Mental Health: An Essay on Psychiatric Social Workers. *280 pp. 1953. 21s.*

Hall, M. Penelope. The Social Services of Modern England. *416 pp. 5th edition (revised) 1960. 28s.*

Heywood, Jean S. Children in Care: the Development of the Service for the Deprived Child. *256 pp. 1959. 25s.*

Jones, Kathleen. Lunacy, Law and Conscience, 1744-1845: the Social History of the Care of the Insane. *268 pp. 1955. 25s.*
Mental Health and Social Policy, 1845-1959. *264 pp. 1960. 28s.*

Jones, Kathleen and Sidebotham, Roy. Mental Hospitals at Work. *220 pp. 1962. 30s.*

Kastell, Jean. Casework in Child Care. *Foreword by M. Brooke Willis. 320 pp. 1962.*

Rooff, Madeline. Voluntary Societies and Social Policy. *350 pp. 15 tables. 1957. 35s.*

Shenfield, B. E. Social Policies for Old Age: A Review of Social Provision for Old Age in Great Britain. *260 pp. 39 tables. 1957. 25s.*

Trasler, Gordon. In Place of Parents: A Study in Foster Care. *272 pp. 1960. 25s.*

Young, A. F., and Ashton, E. T. British Social Work in the Nineteenth Century. *288 pp. 1956. 25s.*

SOCIOLOGY OF EDUCATION

Banks, Olive. Parity and Prestige in English Secondary Education: a Study in Educational Sociology. *272 pp. 1955. 25s.*

Collier, K. G. The Social Purposes of Education: Personal and Social Values in Education. *268 pp. 1959. (2nd Impression 1962.) 21s.*

Connell, W. F. The Educational Thought and Influence of Matthew Arnold. *With an Introduction by Sir Fred Clarke. 332 pp. 1950. 23s.*

Cumming, Ian. Helvetius: His Life and Place in the History of Educational Thought. *With an Introduction by Nicholas Hans. 288 pp. Frontispiece. 1 folder. 1955. 25s.*

Dale, R. R. From School to University: A Study with special reference to University Entrance. *288 pp. 23 tables. 1954. 21s.*

Evans, K. M. Sociometry and Education. *158 pp. 1962. 18s.*

Gasset, José Ortega y. Mission of the University. *Translated with an Introduction by Howard Lee Nostrand. 104 pp. 1946. (2nd Impression 1952.) 12s. 6d.*

Hans, Nicholas. New Trends in Education in the Eighteenth Century. *278 pp. 19 tables. 1951. 25s.*
Comparative Education: A Study of Educational Factors and Traditions. *360 pp. 3rd (revised) edition 1958. (2nd Impression 1961.) 23s.*

Jacks, M. L. Total Education: A Plea for Synthesis. *184 pp. 1946. (4th Impression 1955.) 16s.*

Mannheim, Karl and Stewart, W. A. C. An Introduction to the Sociology of Education. *208 pp. 1962. 21s.*

Ottaway, A. K. C. Education and Society: An Introduction to the Sociology of Education. *With an Introduction by W. O. Lester Smith. 212 pp. 1953. (4th Impression 1960.) 18s.*

Peers, Robert. Adult Education: A Comparative Study. *398 pp. 2nd edition 1959. 35s.*

Samuel, R. H., and Thomas, R. Hinton. Education and Society in Modern Germany. *212 pp. 1949. 16s.*

Wittlin, Alma S. The Museum: Its History and its Tasks in Education. *328 pp. 24 plates. 18 figures. 1949. 28s.*

SOCIOLOGY OF CULTURE

Fromm, Erich. The Fear of Freedom. *286 pp. 1942. (8th Impression 1960.) 21s.* The Sane Society. *400 pp. 1956. (2nd Impression 1959.) 28s.*

Mannheim, Karl. Diagnosis of Our Time: Wartime Essays of a Sociologist. *208 pp. 1943. (7th Impression 1962.) 18s.*
Essays on the Sociology of Culture. *Edited by Ernst Mannheim in co-operation with Paul Kecskemeti. Editorial Note by Adolph Lowe. 280 pp. 1956. (2nd Impression 1962.) 28s.*

Weber, Alfred. Farewell to European History: or The Conquest of Nihilism. *Translated from the German by R. F. C. Hull. 224 pp. 1947. 18s.*

SOCIOLOGY OF RELIGION

Argyle, Michael. Religious Behaviour. *224 pp. 8 figures. 41 tables. 1958. 25s.*

Knight, Frank H., and Merriam, Thornton W. The Economic Order and Religion. *242 pp. 1947. 18s.*

Watt, W. Montgomery. Islam and the Integration of Society. *320 pp. 1961. (2nd Impression.) 32s.*

SOCIOLOGY OF ART AND LITERATURE

Beljame, Alexandre. Men of Letters and the English Public in the Eighteenth Century: 1660-1744, Dryden, Addison, Pope. *Edited with an Introduction and Notes by Bonamy Dobree. Translated by E. O. Lorimer. 532 pp. 1948. 32s.*

Bruford, W. H. Chekhov and His Russia: a Sociological Study. *256 pp. 1948. 18s.*

Misch, Georg. A History of Autobiography in Antiquity. *Translated by E. W. Dickes. 2 Volumes. Vol. 1, 364 pp., Vol. 2, 372 pp. 1950. 45s. the set.*

SOCIOLOGY OF KNOWLEDGE

Hodges, H. A. The Philosophy of Wilhelm Dilthey. *410 pp. 1952. 30s.*

Mannheim, Karl. Essays on the Sociology of Knowledge. *Edited by Paul Kecskemeti. Editorial note by Adolph Lowe. 352 pp. 1952. (2nd Impression 1959.) 35s.*

Schlesinger, Rudolf. Marx: His Time and Ours. *464 pp. 1950. (2nd Impression 1951.) 32s.*

Stark, W. The History of Economics in its Relation to Social Development. *104 pp. 1944. (4th Impression 1957.) 12s.*
America: Ideal and Reality. The United States of 1776 in Contemporary Philosophy. *136 pp. 1947. 12s.*
The Sociology of Knowledge: An Essay in Aid of a Deeper Understanding of the History of Ideas. *384 pp. 1958. (2nd Impression 1960.) 36s.*
Montesquieu: Pioneer of the Sociology of Knowledge. *244 pp. 1960. 25s.*

URBAN SOCIOLOGY

Anderson, Nels. The Urban Community: A World Perspective. *532 pp. 1960. 35s.*

Ashworth, William. The Genesis of Modern British Town Planning: A Study in Economic and Social History of the Nineteenth and Twentieth Centuries. *288 pp. 1954. 25s.*

Cullingworth, J. B. Housing Needs and Planning Policy: A Restatement of the Problems of Housing Need and "Overspill" in England and Wales. *232 pp. 44 tables. 8 maps. 1960. 28s.*

Dickinson, Robert E. City Region and Regionalism: A Geographical Contribution to Human Ecology. *360 pp. 75 figures. 1947. (4th Impression 1960.) 25s.*
The West European City: A Geographical Interpretation. *600 pp. 129 maps. 29 plates. 2nd edition 1962. 55s.*

Dore, R. P. City Life in Japan: A Study of a Tokyo Ward. *498 pp. 8 plates. 4 figures. 24 tables. 1958. 45s.*

Glass, Ruth (Ed.). The Social Background of a Plan: A Study of Middlesbrough. *Preface by Max Lock. 298 pp. 37 tables. 21 folder maps and graphs in pocket. 1948. 42s.*

Gutkind, E. A. Revolution of Environment. *Demy 8vo. 476 pp. 32 plates. 60 figures. 3 folder maps. 1946. 32s.*

Jennings, Hilda. Societies in the Making: a Study of Development and Redevelopment within a County Borough. *Foreword by D. A. Clark. 286 pp. 1962. 32s.*

Kerr, Madeline. The People of Ship Street. *240 pp. 1958. 23s.*

Orlans, Harold. Stevenage: A Sociological Study of a New Town. *344 pp. 1 figure. 3 maps. 1952. 30s.*

RURAL SOCIOLOGY
(*Demy 8vo.*)

Bracey, H. E. English Rural Life: Village Activities, Organizations and Institutions. *302 pp. 1959. 30s.*

Infield, Henrik F. Co-operative Living in Palestine. *With a Foreword by General Sir Arthur Wauchope, G.C.B. 170 pp. 8 plates. 7 tables. 1946. 12s. 6d.*
Co-operative Communities at Work. *204 pp. 15 tables. 1947. 18s.*

Saville, John. Rural Depopulation in England and Wales, 1851-1951. *Foreword by Leonard Elmhirst. 286 pp. 6 figures. 39 tables. 1 map. 1957. 28s. (Dartington Hall Studies in Rural Sociology.)*

Williams, W. M. The Country Craftsman: A Study of Some Rural Crafts and the Rural Industries Organization in England. *248 pp. 9 figures. 1958. 25s. (Dartington Hall Studies in Rural Sociology.)*
The Sociology of an English Village: Gosforth. *272 pp. 12 figures. 13 tables. 1956. (2nd Impression 1956.) 25s.*

SOCIOLOGY OF MIGRATION
(Demy 8vo.)

Eisenstadt, S. N. The Absorption of Immigrants: a Comparative Study based mainly on the Jewish Community in Palestine and the State of Israel. *288 pp. 1954. 25s.*

Little, Dr. K. L. Negroes in Britain: A Study of Racial Relations in English Society. *320 pp. 1947. 25s.*

Richmond, Anthony H. Colour Prejudice in Britain: A Study of West Indian Workers in Liverpool, 1941-1951. *212 pp. 3 figures. 25 tables. 1954. 18s.*

SOCIOLOGY OF INDUSTRY AND DISTRIBUTION
(Demy 8vo.)

Anderson, Nels. Work and Leisure. *280 pp. 1961. 28s.*

Gouldner, Alvin W. Patterns of Industrial Bureaucracy. *298 pp. 1955. 21s.*
Wildcat Strike: A Study of an Unofficial Strike. *202 pp. 10 figures. 1955. 16s.*

Jefferys, Margot, with the assistance of Winifred Moss. Mobility in the Labour Market: Employment Changes in Battersea and Dagenham. *Preface by Barbara Wootton. 186 pp. 51 tables. 1954. 15s.*

Levy, A. B. Private Corporations and Their Control. *Two Volumes. Vol. 1, 464 pp., Vol. 2, 432 pp. 1950. 80s. the set.*

Levy, Hermann. The Shops of Britain: A Study of Retail Distribution. *268 pp. 1948. (2nd Impression 1949.) 21s.*

Liepmann, Kate. The Journey to Work: Its Significance for Industrial and Community Life. *With a Foreword by A. M. Carr-Saunders. 230 pp. 40 tables. 3 folders. 1944. (2nd Impression 1945.) 18s.*
Apprenticeship: An Enquiry into its Adequacy under Modern Conditions. *Foreword by H. D. Dickinson. 232 pp. 6 tables. 1960. (2nd Impression.) 23s.*

Smelser, Neil J. Social Change in the Industrial Revolution: An Application of Theory to the Lancashire Cotton Industry, 1770-1840. *468 pp. 12 figures. 14 tables. 1959. (2nd Impression 1960.) 40s.*

Williams, Gertrude. Recruitment to Skilled Trades. *240 pp. 1957. 23s.*

ANTHROPOLOGY
(Demy 8vo.)

Crook, David and Isabel. Revolution in a Chinese Village: Ten Mile Inn. *230 pp. 8 plates. 1 map. 1959. 21s.*

Dube, S. C. Indian Village, *Foreword by Morris Edward Opler. 276 pp. 4 plates. 1955. (4th Impression 1961.) 25s.*
India's Changing Villages: Human Factors in Community Development. *260 pp. 8 plates. 1 map. 1958. (2nd Impression 1960.) 25s.*

Fei, Hsiao-Tung. Peasant Life in China. *Foreword by Bronislaw Malinowski. 320 pp. 14 plates. 1939. (5th Impression 1962.) 30s.*

Fei, Hsiao-Tung and Chang, Chih-I. Earthbound China: A Study of Rural Economy in Yunnan. *Revised English edition prepared in collaboration with Paul Cooper and Margaret Park Redfield. 346 pp. 7 plates. 50 tables. 1948. 20s.*

Gulliver, P. H. The Family Herds. A Study of Two Pastoral Tribes in East Africa, The Jie and Turkana. *304 pp. 4 plates. 19 figures. 1955. 25s.*

Hogbin, Ian. Transformation Scene. The Changing Culture of a New Guinea Village. *340 pp. 22 plates. 2 maps. 1951. 30s.*

Hsu, Francis L. K. Under the Ancestors' Shadow: Chinese Culture and Personality. *346 pp. 26 figures. 1949. 21s.*
Religion, Science and Human Crises: A Study of China in Transition and its Implications for the West. *168 pp. 7 figures. 4 tables. 1952. 16s.*

Kelsen, Hans. Society and Nature: A Sociological Inquiry. *414 pp. 1946. 25s.*

Lin Yueh-Hwa. The Golden Wing: A Sociological Study of Chinese Familism. *Introduced by Raymond Firth. 264 pp. 1947. 18s.*

Lowie, Professor Robert H. Social Organization. *494 pp. 1950. (3rd Impression 1962.) 35s.*

Maunier, René. The Sociology of Colonies: An Introduction to the Study of Race Contact. *Edited and translated by E. O. Lorimer. 2 Volumes. Vol. 1, 430 pp., Vol. 2, 356 pp. 1949. 70s. the set.*

Mayer, Adrian C. Caste and Kinship in Central India: A Village and its Region. *328 pp. 16 plates. 15 figures. 16 tables. 1960. 35s.*
Peasants in the Pacific: A Study of Fiji Indian Rural Society. *232 pp. 16 plates. 10 figures. 14 tables. 1961. 35s.*

Osborne, Harold. Indians of the Andes: Aymaras and Quechuas. *292 pp. 8 plates. 2 maps. 1952. 25s.*

Smith, Raymond T. The Negro Family in British Guiana: Family Structure and Social Status in the Villages. *With a Foreword by Meyer Fortes. 314 pp. 8 plates. 1 figure. 4 maps. 1956. 28s.*

Yang, Martin C. A Chinese Village: Taitou, Shantung Province. *Foreword by Ralph Linton. Introduction by M. L. Wilson. 308 pp. 1947. 23s.*

DOCUMENTARY
(*Demy 8vo.*)

Belov, Fedor. The History of a Soviet Collective Farm. *250 pp. 1956. 21s.*

Meek, Dorothea L. (Ed.). Soviet Youth: Some Achievements and Problems. *Excerpts from the Soviet Press, translated by the editor. 280 pp. 1957. 28s.*

Schlesinger, Rudolf (Ed.). Changing Attitudes in Soviet Russia.
1. The Family in the U.S.S.R. *Documents and Readings, with an Introduction by the editor. 434 pp. 1949. 30s.*
2. The Nationalities Problem and Soviet Administration. Selected Readings on the Development of Soviet Nationalities Policies. *Introduced by the editor. Translated by W. W. Gottlieb. 324 pp. 1956. 30s.*

Reports
of the Institute
# of Community Studies

(Demy 8vo.)

Jackson, Brian and **Marsden, Dennis**. Education and the Working Class: Some General Themes raised by a Study of 88 Working-class Children in a Northern Industrial City. *268 pp. 2 folders. 1962. 28s.*

Marris, Peter. Widows and their Families. *Foreword by Dr. John Bowlby. 184 pp. 18 tables. Statistical Summary. 1958. 18s.*
Family and Social Change in an African City. A Study of Rehousing in Lagos. *196 pp. 1 map. 4 plates. 53 tables. 1961. 25s.*

Mills, Enid. Living with Mental Illness: a Study in East London. *Foreword by Morris Carstairs. 196 pp. 1962. 28s.*

Townsend, Peter. The Family Life of Old People: An Inquiry in East London. *Foreword by J. H. Sheldon. 300 pp. 3 figures. 63 tables. 1957. (2nd Impression 1961.) 30s.*

Willmott, Peter and **Young, Michael**. Family and Class in a London Suburb. *202 pp. 47 tables. 1960. (2nd Impression 1961.) 21s.*

Young, Michael and **Willmott, Peter**. Family and Kinship in East London. *Foreword by Richard M. Titmuss. 252 pp. 39 tables. 1957.*

The British Journal of Sociology. *Edited by D. G. MacRae. Vol. 1, No. 1, March 1950 and Quarterly. Roy. 8vo., £2 12s. 6d. a number, post free. (Vols. 1-10, £3 each.)*

All prices are net and subject to alteration without notice